UNEMPLOYMENT

and the American Economy

ARTHUR M. ROSS, Editor

*One of a series of books from the
Research Program on Unemployment
Arthur M. Ross and R. A. Gordon, Directors*

*Institute of Industrial Relations
University of California, Berkeley*

JOHN WILEY & SONS, INC.

NEW YORK · LONDON · SYDNEY

Library of Congress Catalog Card Number: 64-14999
Printed in the United States of America

Contributors

E. Wight Bakke, Director, Labor-Management Center, and Sterling Professor of Economics, Yale University

Jack Downie (deceased, August 1963), Late Chief Economist, Organization for Economic Cooperation and Development, Paris, France

Otto Eckstein, Professor of Economics and Managing Editor, *Review of Economics and Statistics,* Harvard University

Robben W. Fleming, Professor of Law, University of Illinois; former Director, Institute of Labor and Industrial Relations, University of Illinois

Nathaniel Goldfinger, Director, Department of Research, AFL-CIO

William Haber, Dean, College of Literature, Science and the Arts, University of Michigan, Ann Arbor

Walter W. Heller, Chairman, Council of Economic Advisers; former Chairman, Department of Economics, University of Minnesota

vii

Richard A. Lester, Chairman, Department of Economics, and Faculty Associate of the Industrial Relations Section, Princeton University

Paul W. McCracken, Professor of Business Administration, University of Michigan; former Member, Council of Economic Advisers

William H. Miernyk, Director, Bureau of Economic Research, University of Colorado

Robert J. Myers, Deputy Commissioner, Bureau of Labor Statistics, U. S. Department of Labor; former Chief of Statistical Bureau, International Labour Office, Geneva

Albert Rees, Chairman, Department of Economics, University of Chicago

Arthur M. Ross, Professor of Industrial Relations; former Director, Institute of Industrial Relations, University of California, Berkeley

Gerald G. Somers, Professor of Economics, University of Wisconsin; former Director, Institute of Industrial Relations, West Virginia University

Don Vial, Director of Research and Administrative Assistant to the Secretary-Treasurer, California Federation of Labor, AFL-CIO

Seymour L. Wolfbein, Director, Office of Manpower, Automation and Training, U. S. Department of Labor

Foreword

During 1962 a four-year program of research and conferences on the subject of Unemployment and the American Economy was initiated at the University of California. This program is based on the conviction that unemployment will continue to be the most serious and pressing domestic economic problem of the 1960's. The Ford Foundation made a generous grant to the Institute of Industrial Relations at the Berkeley campus of the University of California to support the work.

The undersigned, who were serving as Director of the Institute and Chairman of the Economics Department, respectively, at the time of the grant, became co-directors of the unemployment program. Although we have since given up our administrative positions, we agreed to remain in charge of the program until its conclusion.

Our research projects and conferences are based on the premise that persistent unemployment calls for new policies, both public and private, with which we have had little previous experience in the United States. More adequate information on labor force

and occupational trends is needed in order to guide the movement of workers from one area to another and the retraining of
workers for different occupations. Factors which make for success or failure in training, retraining, and area redevelopment
must be identified. New experiments in collective bargaining over
problems of labor adjustment require careful study. The possibilities and limitations of tax cuts, "wage restraint," and other
general economic policies must be clarified.

To meet these needs, we are conducting a coordinated group
of studies designed to furnish better guidelines for the development of policy in these relatively unfamiliar areas, and to provide
critical evaluation of the policies as they are established and implemented during the next several years. The project also includes
closely related studies designed to clarify the question of what
our employment goals should be and facilitate more accurate
prediction of labor market trends in the next decade or so. The
studies are being conducted by economists and sociologists on
the Berkeley campus of the University of California, by doctoral
candidates, and by several economists in eastern universities who
have become associated with the project since the original plans
were developed.

Another element in our program is an annual conference on
unemployment, which brings together key people involved in
research, policy formulation, and administration. The first of these
conferences was held at the Claremont Hotel, Berkeley, April 18–
20, 1963. Conferees included about seventy-five scholars, government officials, and representatives of management, labor, and
community organizations from various parts of the country. In
addition, several hundred persons attended the morning sessions,
which were open to the public, as well as the dinner on April 19,
which was addressed by Governor Edmund G. Brown of California.

The second of our annual conferences will be held at Boulder,
Colorado, in June of 1964.

This book consists of the papers and comments delivered during
the formal sessions of the 1963 conference on Unemployment and
the American Economy. Believing that the issues discussed on
that occasion are still very much alive, we decided that these
important statements by leading figures in governmental, aca-

demic, and private life should be made available to a wider public.

Arthur M. Ross
Professor of Industrial Relations

R. A. Gordon
Professor of Economics

University of California, Berkeley
January 1964

Contents

CHAPTER 1

Introduction

BY ARTHUR M. ROSS

The Problem of Unemployment

The causes of excessive unemployment may be uncertain; its effects are not. The lack of economic opportunity has led to demoralization and delinquency among large numbers of young people. Prolonged joblessness has had a catastrophic effect in the families of displaced miners and industrial workers, some of whom have had only a little casual work during the past several years. Unemployment is one of the key factors in the current racial crisis. The issue of job security lies behind most of our difficult labor management disputes in the 1960's.

The economic impact is also clear enough. Between 1958 and 1962, it has been estimated, the cumulative excess of *potential* over *actual* output in the United States came to $170 billion in 1962 prices, or approximately $3,000 for every family. Secretary of Labor Wirtz has said, repeatedly, that more working time was lost in 1962 because of unemployment alone than has been incurred in labor disputes since the government first began to publish strike statistics in 1927.

President Kennedy referred to unemployment as "a national disgrace." In March 1963 he stated that "our No. 1 domestic concern is, and must be . . . jobs for the tidal wave of men and women now flooding our labor market."

Who are the unemployed? The best-known measure of joblessness in the United States is the Labor Department's "unemployment rate," showing the percentage of the civilian labor force without work. Like the Dow-Jones average and the Consumer Price Index, the unemployment rate receives widespread notice as a symbol of the economic situation.

Historically the overall rate has been subject to extreme fluctuations. At one point during the 1930's it exceeded 25 per cent, while it fell to less than 1 per cent during the Second World War. The variations have been narrower in the postwar period, however, ranging from 2.5 per cent in 1953 to 6.8 per cent in 1958. One disturbing fact is that, although recent business cycles have been relatively mild, periods of recovery have increasingly fallen short of full employment. The unemployment rate stood at 2.5 per cent in 1953, at 3.8 per cent in 1956, at 5.5 per cent in 1959, and at 5.6 per cent in 1962. And, after more than two years of strenuous effort to "get the country running," the Kennedy Administration still confronted a rate of 5.7 per cent in June 1963.

Despite the simplicity and popularity of this single ratio, it is not adequate for all the purposes of unemployment data. Among these purposes are: to reveal the proportion of our manpower resources not contributing to national output, to assess the extent of hardship because of unemployment, and to provide guidance for economic and labor market policies. The need for more detailed measures of the structure of unemployment was strongly emphasized in the recent report of the President's Committee to Appraise Employment and Unemployment Statistics.

Thus, many people argue that unemployment is not so serious a problem for housewives with working husbands, or for young people attempting to break into the labor market, as it is for married men with families to support. Among the approximately 4,000,000 unemployed in May 1963, about 1,100,000 were single persons under 20 years of age. Another 680,000 were married women living with their husbands. Some 1,500,000 were heads of households, of whom 1,100,000 were men. Specific unemployment rates among these groups varied from 3.0 per cent for the married men to 18.9 per cent for the single persons under 20.

Many other differentials must be noted if we are to have a reliable picture of the problem. Unemployment rates gradually decrease with advancing age. Among women the decline is unbroken, since older women tend to leave the labor market if jobs are unavailable. With men the lowest percentage of unemployment is in the 35–44 age bracket, beyond which the rate increases. Long-term unemployment is more serious for older workers than for any other group, however. In May 1963, for instance, almost 50 per cent of unemployed men over 45 years of age had been out of work for 15 weeks or more.

Nonwhite workers suffer a disproportionate incidence of unemployment, the rates being approximately double those of the white workers. Limited education, low levels of skill and experience, and job discrimination often combine to yield particularly high rates for Negroes. A recent survey in Oakland, California, showed some precincts with more than one-third of the Negroes out of work.

Then there are important occupational and industrial differentials. While only 1.4 per cent of managers, officials, and proprietors, and 3.7 per cent of clerical and sales workers, were unemployed in May 1963, the corresponding figures were 7.5 per cent for semiskilled and 11.0 per cent for unskilled industrial workers. Likewise the rate varied from 2.9 per cent for persons who last worked in government jobs to 9.6 per cent for construction workers.

Finally, the personal and social effects of unemployment depend, to a very large extent, on its duration. If 1,000 workers are each out of work for three weeks, this does not create much of a problem although it contributes to the statistics. But, if 100 workers are each unemployed for 30 weeks, there will undoubtedly be real deprivation and erosion of living standards although in one sense the overall statistical effect will be the same. For this reason, data on long-term unemployment are particularly significant. Government reports show that approximately 30 per cent of unemployed workers had been out of work for 15 weeks or more as of May 1963; about 16 per cent had been jobless for 27 weeks or more. It is distressing that the proportion of long-term unemployed among the total has tended to rise in recent years. At the center of the problem are the "hard-core" unemployed who, because of a combination of disadvantageous circumstances, are the most difficult to integrate into the labor force and who, in some cases, have been forced to accept unemployment as a more or less permanent way of life.

Characterizing the incidence of unemployment as a whole, the Department of Labor has this to say:

. . . While it would be desirable to reduce joblessness among all groups in the labor force, the most serious, persistent and intractable unemployment problems are those of (1) young people, (2) older workers, (3) non-white workers, (4) the relatively unskilled, and (5) workers attached to declining industries or to those characterized by highly seasonal or otherwise unstable employment. For those unfortunate workers who fall in more than one of these groups the problems are, of course, intensified.[1]

Is unemployment a serious problem? Obviously, then, unemployment is not a homogeneous phenomenon. A young electrical engineer who spends a few weeks after graduating from M.I.T. in the enjoyable pastime of playing off would-be employers against each other is unemployed. A former coal miner in West Virginia who has long since exhausted his unemployment insurance and has fallen into utter destitution is also unemployed. Moreover, there are admitted conceptual difficulties in defining unemployment as well as statistical difficulties in counting it. Under these circumstances it was predictable that arguments would be offered to the effect that unemployment is largely a statistical illusion.

Allegations of bad faith or incompetency in the collection of statistics have long since been effectively laid to rest. Knowledgeable observers of every political persuasion are in agreement that the facts are gathered honestly and carefully. The real problems are those of definition and method, areas in which capable professionals may differ legitimately.

An unemployed person, of course, is one who is out of work, able to work, and looking for work. If a person is unable to work, or not looking for work, he is not in the labor force and therefore not unemployed. Although these concepts can be stated simply, they are not always easy to apply. In practice the most difficult problem is to decide whether a given individual is looking hard enough as to be actively in the labor market for statistical purposes. The interviewers count as unemployed those who have made job-seeking efforts during the survey week; those who are awaiting the results of recent efforts such as letters of application; those on layoff who are waiting to be called back to their jobs; those who are waiting to report to a new job which is scheduled to commence in the near future; and those who "would have been looking for work except that they were temporarily ill or believed no work was available in their line of work or in the community."

Inevitably the last criterion includes subjective and speculative elements, reflecting the fact that the border of the labor force is not really a definite line but a shifting and shadowy area. The President's Committee to Appraise Employment and Unemployment Statistics ("Gordon Committee") has recommended that a more definite appraisal of the quality or sufficiency of job-seeking efforts be made by the interviewers.

While recognizing that some individuals may currently be counted as unemployed although they are not really looking very hard, the Gordon Committee notes two factors which work in the opposite direction. First, some people—married women in particular—retire from the labor force although they would prefer to be working if jobs were available. Perhaps such persons should be counted as unemployed, but if this were done the concept of unemployment would be even more subjective and less behavioral. Second, involuntary part-time employment and "underemployment" are not counted in the usual statistics.

The extent of part-time work in the American economy is quite surprising: in 1962 more than 11,000,000 nonagricultural employees had schedules of less than 35 hours per week. In about two-thirds of the cases, part-time employment was voluntary in the sense that the workers did not want full-time jobs. As the number of students, working women, and older persons still in good health continues to rise, voluntary part-time work will undoubtedly increase as well. At the same time the expansion of trade and service industries will provide more part-time jobs. (Incidentally, most of the increase in wage and salary employment since 1957 has consisted of additional part-time jobs in the trade and service industries. Periodic announcements that "employment in the United States has reached an all-time high" gives a somewhat misleading impression of manpower utilization.)

Involuntary part-time employment results principally from slack business and inability to find a full-time job. In 1962 an average of 2,300,000 nonagricultural employees worked part-time for these economic reasons. This factor adds about one percentage point to the unemployment rate. Thus the rate was 5.9 per cent in May 1963, but the proportion of "labor force time lost through unemployment and [involuntary] part-time work" was 6.9 per cent.

Underemployment may be defined as employment which is relatively unproductive and unrewarding in comparison with normal levels of productivity in the economy and with the real capacities of the individuals involved. A highly skilled mechanic is underemployed if he is compelled to perform unskilled labor for lack of opportunity in his regular trade. A house-to-house salesman peddling a product for which there is virtually no demand is similarly underemployed, as is a college-trained Negro who must operate an elevator because of job discrimination. Underemployment is characteristic of agricultural economies in the early stages of development. There is relatively little full-time unemployment in India, for example, but a vast underutilization of agricultural manpower. In an advanced economy such as the United States, underemployment is not so serious a national problem, yet it certainly is endemic in southern agriculture and various urban pursuits. So far no one has been successful in measuring the extent of underemployment or the economic loss resulting therefrom, but the fact that a phenomenon cannot be measured does not make it unimportant.

Despite these conceptual and statistical problems of measuring unemployment, the Gordon Committee concluded that "the concept of unemployment now in official use is a reasonable one and represents a conscientious and well-designed effort over a long period of time to resolve a wide range of difficult issues." [2] Thus the problem of unemployment is not a statistical illusion and *is* clearly serious.

Comparison of unemployment in the United States with that in Western Europe and Japan serves to confirm this statement.

In recent years our rates of unemployment have been two to three times as high as the average of other advanced industrial nations, and four to six times as high as those in Germany and Japan. Contrary to widespread impressions, these persistent differentials cannot be accounted for by differences in statistical concepts and techniques.

Finally, the magnitude of the problem can be measured by asking how many additional jobs would have to be created in order to achieve the objective of full employment. The issue of whether this objective should be defined in terms of a 3 per cent rate, a 4 per cent rate, or cannot be expressed by a single figure will be sidestepped here, and for purposes of discussion the more conservative 4 per cent rate will be used. Dr. Gerhard Colm of the National Planning Association has calculated that 5,600,000 new jobs would have to be created during 1963 in order to cut the unemployment rate to 4 per cent by the end of the year. Among the components of this estimate were (a) 1,500,000 "replacement jobs" to absorb the workers who would be displaced by mechanization, other technological changes, and improved organization and management; (b) 1,200,000 jobs to absorb the net increase in the labor force; (c) 1,100,000 jobs to reduce the unemployment rate to 4 per cent; (d) 1,000,000 full-time equivalent jobs to offset involuntary part-time unemployment; and (e) 800,000 jobs for workers who had recently left the labor force because of unfavorable prospects and who could be expected to re-enter if conditions improved.[3]

Dr. Colm's figures are consistent with the estimate by the Council of Economic Advisers, discussed in Part II of this volume, that 3,100,000 new jobs would be needed to reduce the unemployment rate to a 4 per cent level by the end of 1963. The difference is explained by the fact that the Council's estimate does not include "replacement jobs" and does not provide for the elimination of involuntary part-time unemployment.

But, since the beginning of the current recovery period early in 1961, civilian employment has been increasing at a rate of only slightly more than 1,000,000 jobs per year. This means that, aside from "replacement jobs" to offset rising productivity, the normal increase in the labor force is barely being met. Nothing is being done to reduce the unemployment rate, which has remained virtually unchanged; to permit the re-entry of those who have left the labor force for lack of opportunity; or to provide full-time work for involuntary part-time workers.

Thus, although much effort is expended in debating how the full-employment objective should be defined, practically no progress is being made in attaining even the more conservative definition of the objective.

What Are the Causes of Unemployment?

Normal unemployment. A cross-sectional view of the labor market at any point of time would show a picture of great animation. Each month several million persons enter or re-enter the labor force; almost as many leave. Several million more are laid off by their employers, or discharged for cause, or voluntarily elect to change their jobs. Some industries are experiencing a seasonal lull; others are moving into the busy season. While some firms are expanding, others are going out of business. Meanwhile individuals and families are moving about the country, principally into Los Angeles but elsewhere in lesser degree.

Since these movements inevitably take a certain amount of time, there will always be unemployed workers representing normal processes of change in the labor market. This is the unemployment which causes little concern in time of peace, and which is consistent with the concept of full employment. Sometimes it is called the "irreducible minimum," although that term is rather misleading.

To calculate the amount or rate of normal or "frictional" unemployment is not a simple undertaking. As already mentioned, the rate was reduced to less than 1 per cent during the Second World War, but at that time extraordinary manpower controls were in effect and the public employment service was playing an unusually active role in the economy.

The Bureau of Labor Statistics has presented estimates of normal unemployment in the 1955–1957 period. The overall unemployment rate averaged slightly more than 4 per cent during that period, and the BLS concludes that short-term frictional unemployment accounted for 2.5 per cent, leaving about 1.7 per cent to be explained by other reasons. Among the major components were seasonal fluctuations, entry or re-entry into the labor market, voluntary labor turnover, and adjustment to long-term economic changes.[4] In view of increasing numbers of young persons, older workers, and females in the labor force, BLS foresaw that the level of frictional unemployment might rise to 3.0 per cent in 1975. As Professor Eckstein points out in Chapter 5 of this volume, 3.0 per cent is considerably less than 4.0 per cent, which the Kennedy Administration originally advanced as a definition of full employment and later characterized as an "interim target."

Actually it is doubtful that normal unemployment can be expressed numerically without reference to the state of the economy. The length of time required to effect routine job changes obviously varies with business conditions. Young people entering the labor market can find work more easily when jobs are plentiful. The construction industry is more seasonal in bad times than in good times. And the fact that several European countries have been able to hold unemployment below 2.0 per cent for long periods of time suggests that it may be fallacious to regard 2.5 or 3.0 per cent as an "irreducible minimum," although it is conceded that there are differences in educational systems and other institutions which affect these comparisons.

The issue of structural unemployment. At any rate it is clear that unemployment in the United States has been well above the irreducible minimum, however that might be defined, for a large number of years. Debate concerning the causes of this problem has centered on the issue of structural versus aggregative causes.

According to the structuralists, the principal explanation of persistent unemployment in recent years has been the rapid transformation of economic activity and occupational structure. They point to the declining importance of goods-producing industries and the growth of service-rendering industries including government, education, and finance. They emphasize the shrinkage of blue-collar occupations and the expansion of white-collar, technical, and professional employment. They also note the changes in the geographical pattern of economic activity. As a result of all these changes, they state, imbalances have developed between labor demand and labor supply. Many displaced workers do not have the right education, the right skills, and the right employment experience to qualify for the new jobs becoming available. Geographical immobility adds to the problem. Consequently there are shortages of engineers, teachers, nurses, and secretaries while displaced coal miners, meat packers, and steel workers remain out of work indefinitely.

The aggregative theorists (including Dr. Heller and Professor Eckstein, whose essays are included in this volume) recognize the existence of structural *differentials* in unemployment. Blue-collar workers, young persons, and employees of manufacturing and construction industries are more likely to be out of work than professional workers, middle-aged persons, and employees of governmental agencies. But these differentials have *always* existed; and the aggregative theorists contend that they have not become any more pronounced since 1957, when the generally favorable employment situation of the postwar period took a turn for the worse. Moreover, they point out that the trend of productivity increases did not accelerate after 1957; that there is no evidence of declining geographical mobility; and that after 1957 the number of job openings appears to have fallen off in every occupational category. The basic cause of recent unemployment, therefore, is not structural transformation but insufficient aggregate demand on the part of consumers, business firms, and government. These arguments were advanced by Edward Kalachek and James Knowles in their influential paper presented to the Joint Economic Committee in 1961. Dr. Heller develops them further in this volume and shows that after 1960 the unemployment rate was reduced significantly in those activities most directly affected by structural change, including mining, durable goods manufacturing, and transportation.

The debate over the causes of recent unemployment has considerable political significance. The structural explanation focuses on the educational system, training institutions, counseling and guidance of young workers, area redevelopment, relocation, and other measures to increase labor mobility. If a pure structuralist could be found, he would argue that there are enough jobs to go around and that the real problem is one of matching labor demand and labor supply. The aggregative explanation calls for policies to increase effective demand, expansionary fiscal and monetary policies in particular. If a pure aggregative theorist could be found, he would point to our Second World War experience and argue that, if the jobs are available, workers will manage to find them and to qualify for them. In general, Congress has been more sympathetic to the structural solutions up to the present time.

Undoubtedly the debate will continue as further research on the structure of unemployment is conducted. The consensus of professional, as distinguished from Congressional, opinion probably favors the aggregative explanation at the moment, but it must be said that Heller, Knowles, Kalachek, and others have reached their conclusions on the basis of rather meager factual data. Studies limited to changes since 1957, and dealing with large aggregates such as "blue-collar workers" and "goods-producing industries" cannot be considered very definitive. Other aspects of the structure of employment are now being studied, and longer periods of time are being taken into account. It seems clear that the proportion of long-term unemployed among total unemployed has been increasing; those out of work for 27 weeks or more rose from 6 per cent of the total in May 1949 to 19 per cent in May 1961.[5] Evidence is also accumulating that unemployment rates of Negroes are increasing relative to the total.

Until better information on job vacancies is available, it will be impossible to know, with certainty, whether a great many unfilled jobs exist for which qualified applicants cannot be found or which they will not accept. Thus inevitably the debate is rather inconclusive.

Deficiency of demand. Whether or not deficiency of demand is the paramount cause, it is clearly an important cause of recent unemployment. It is not that production has declined; on the contrary, every year since 1950 has set a record Gross National Product in dollar terms, and every year except two has set a new high in real terms. But the increase has not been great enough to balance the rise in productivity, which reduces labor demand per unit of output, and the growth in the working population, which of course constitutes additional labor supply. "Growth rate" expresses these relationships in shorthand: if output per capita is rising 3.0 per cent per year, and the working population 1.5 per cent, then real GNP must increase about 4.5 per cent annually or unemployment will increase. Growth rates lend themselves to political disputation since they can be manipulated unmercifully by choice of convenient time periods. For example,

Republicans could accurately claim a growth rate of 7.0 per cent in 1959, using the previous year as a base, while Democrats with equal accuracy could point to an average annual growth of 2.4 per cent since 1953. In any event, production has not been rising fast enough. The average annual rate of growth during the 1950's was about 3.3 per cent, and unemployment grew more serious. And although GNP (in 1962 prices) increased from $516 billion in 1960 to $554 billion in 1962, or about 5 per cent per year, the unemployment rate was still 5.5 per cent at the end of the period. Economic growth continued at approximately the same speed in the early months of 1963; the unemployment rate rose to 5.7 per cent in June.

The principal components of GNP are consumer expenditures, private investment, and government purchases of goods and services. Consumer spending has increased at a substantial rate since the mid-1950's, government spending has fluctuated, but private investment has lagged badly. More information is needed to account for the virtual stagnation of private investment. Has the long-term decline in the capital-output ratio—the trend away from the more massive types of investment characteristic of the pre-Second World War period—been a contributing factor? Is the United States in the downswing of a long construction cycle reflecting special influences such as population growth, family formation, and housing supply? Or should the blame be placed on the profit squeeze and lack of "business confidence"?

It is clear that, if production is sufficiently accelerated to restore full employment, the stimulus will have to come from private investment, or government fiscal operations, or some combination of the two. The consumers will respond to any such stimulus and will probably spend about 93 cents out of every dollar of additional income; but, because of the nature of the situation, they cannot take the initiative. Dr. Heller estimates that GNP would have to rise by about $16 billion every three months in order to reduce the unemployment rate to 4 per cent by the end of 1964. At the current rate of growth, he points out, it would take at least ten years to achieve this objective.

Automation and unemployment. So much is heard about automation in current discussions of unemployment that one gets the impression of a novel, unique, and terrifying cause at work. Many conferences have been held on the impacts of automation; many research projects have been launched. State legislatures and governors have established commissions on automation; and in July 1963 President Kennedy announced his intention of appointing a presidential commission, composed of "the ablest men in public and private life," which will "undertake the most comprehensive review of this complex and many-sided subject ever ventured."

The term "automation" originally signified certain advanced technologies involving continuous processes, numerical controls, the feedback principle, and so on. But popular usage eventually swamped this restricted definition, until "automation" has come to mean virtually every kind of technological, organizational, and economic change resulting in displacement of workers. Thus President Kennedy stated that one of the responsibilities of his Commission on Automation would be "identifying and describing the major types of worker displacement, *both technological and economic,* which are likely to occur during the next ten years." (Emphasis added.) It is significant that the most drastic employment declines (such as in the railroad and coal-mining industries) have *not* resulted from the introduction of automation in the original specialized sense.

Putting old wine into new bottles is an ancient and honorable pastime, but sometimes it results in misunderstanding and confusion. There is every reason to study the impacts of change more carefully, anticipate the human problems more intelligently, and share the costs more equitably. If new terminology helps, so be it. Nevertheless it is important to keep in mind that it is a complex of changes—technological, organizational, and industrial—which results in the displacement of workers. If a shorthand designation is needed, "technology" is preferable to "automation" for it can more easily be understood as encompassing the totality of productive techniques and not merely physical techniques.

As more intensive study is made of technology's impact, what has already been learned should not be forgotten. We have learned that almost every technological change is labor-saving in the sense of reducing labor requirements per unit (including the labor required to make the equipment). If this were not true, the additional investment would ordinarily not be economical. We have learned that many workers are displaced or disemployed because of technological change; and, regardless of what the long-run outcome may be, their short-run deprivations are very real. Economic history is replete with piteous cases of workers left stranded because their craft was eliminated, their company went out of business, or their industry declined.

Of course, disemployment does not always result. If the volume of activity in the company is increasing, and the affected workers can be used on the new processes, there may be little or no displacement. Thus office automation has given rise to almost no employment problems in the postwar period despite the drastic reduction of labor requirements per unit in some clerical tasks. The real displacement problems are found where demand is not increasing rapidly enough to absorb the affected workers or where other individuals are brought in to perform the new tasks.

But what about the long run? The controversy about whether technological change causes long-run unemployment has been essentially sterile because the terms of reference have been too limited. The answer cannot be found in the particular industry where changes have been introduced and workers have been displaced. On the contrary, it must be sought in the general process of economic growth out of which new job opportunities are precipitated. It is self-evident that, in order to prevent unemployment from increasing, we need "replacement jobs" to absorb the workers released by technological change as well as additional jobs for new entrants into the labor force.

The fate of the individuals immediately affected is not necessarily determined by the general trend of employment. Even in a period of falling employment, a skilled secretary who is displaced in a company reorganization will probably land on her feet with little difficulty. On the other hand, some of the current unemployed (for example, displaced steel workers and coal miners in late middle age) will probably never have steady jobs again even if a very high rate of growth is attained. This type of labor market analysis is highly elliptical; it helps to predict the *net* effects but tells little or nothing about any given individual. Nevertheless, it remains true that the re-employment prospects of displaced individuals *in general* are vitally affected by the condition of the economy.

These observations about the impact of technological change

are so axiomatic that they have taken on a bromidic quality. Now, is there anything unique or peculiar about the contemporary changes which are lumped together under the rubric of "automation"?

The situation does have some novel aspects, but not those which are frequently attributed to it. For example, while some types of work are disappearing, there is no basis for the idea that work *as such* is vanishing along with the great auk and the buffalo bison. Just as agricultural work was supplanted by industrial work, now industrial work is being supplanted by white-collar, professional, and service work. Notwithstanding Norbert Wiener and other writers of science fiction, a world in which man's only serious responsibility will be that of dutiful consumption is not yet around the corner. In fact, Sebastian DeGrazia has argued that, if working hours are realistically defined (to include commuting time, for example), Americans of today really have little more leisure than did their forebears in the nineteenth century. It is significant that the decline of working hours has slowed down in recent decades; that there is little sentiment for shortening hours among rank and file workers except for those threatened by insecurity; that the proportion of working women has increased greatly; and that millions of Americans practice "moonlighting."

To keep "automation" in perspective, it must be noted also that there has not been any dramatic acceleration in productivity in the past decade, and that productivity has been increasing much more rapidly in Western Europe and Japan than in the United States. Likewise our own history shows that there is no positive correlation between increase in productivity and rate of unemployment.

But the great gap between the declining and the growing occupations is new. In earlier times it was not too difficult for a displaced cotton farmer to go into a textile factory or an auto assembly plant. Today, however, the displaced mill hand or assembler may have little or no chance of moving into the expanding sector of the labor market. Obviously he cannot find work as a teacher, a scientist, or an engineer. For retail selling, secretarial work, nursing, and other expanding occupations below the professional level, he is likely to find himself at the wrong age, of the wrong sex, and with the wrong education. If he is also of the wrong race (and Negro workers have been heavily represented in some declining occupations), his problem is so much the worse. As a result of educational obsolescence, social barriers, age preferences, and racial discrimination, there is a strong tendency to staff the growing occupations and industries with well-educated young white men and women. As displaced workers experience greater difficulty in breaking into the expanding sector, the proportion of long-term unemployed among all unemployed grows ever larger. Thus the problem of the *convertibility of the labor force* has become more serious than in any previous cycle of technological change.

The other novel element in the situation is our greater awareness of it. Facts and figures about unemployment are available to an unprecedented extent; and, as noted above, there have been no end of conferences, commissions, and research projects. It is unlikely that the President of the United States has ever discussed the problem of unemployment so frequently and so urgently in any previous period in which 5 to 6 per cent of the labor force was out of work. Whether or not enough is being done, the country is certainly conscious of unemployment.

The fact is, of course, that the threshold of consciousness of social problems in general has been lowered. At the same time, immensely greater social responsibilities have been accepted by government as the price of political survival. One of the new responsibilities of the federal government is the commitment to maintain high-level employment. Although this commitment does not really enjoy a very high priority in the conduct of national affairs, nevertheless it is part of our law. It could be carried out more seriously. Perhaps the current discussion of "automation," despite all its confusion and waste motion, will contribute to the attainment of this result.

Economic Policies of Government

The commitment to high employment. All governments of advanced industrial nations have assumed some type of formal responsibility for employment. The gradual assumption of this responsibility by the American government provides a striking example of how ideas adjust themselves to circumstances in political life. Until 1929 it was generally believed that a depression was the result of maladjustments in the cost-price structure which must be allowed to work themselves out over the course of time. Government interference, no matter how well intentioned, would only make matters worse. Many even refused to recognize unemployment as a disease of the system as a whole and preferred to regard it as the result of indolence and prodigality. It was assumed that any necessary relief assistance would be supplied through private charitable organizations; each local community and religious group would "care for its own." Government would make its greatest contribution toward recovery by reducing expenditures, finding new sources of revenue, and thus balancing the budget. This action would set a good example for households and private business and maintain confidence in the soundness of the dollar.

The story of government policy during the Hoover Administration is a well-remembered one: the President's unflinching outward cheerfulness; exhortations to employers to keep workers on the payroll and maintain their wage rates; the "Give a Job" campaign of 1931, addressed to the householder, urging him to have his yard cleaned or his cellar whitewashed; the President's refusal to sanction federal relief or public works despite the breakdown of private charity and local public assistance; the establishment of the RFC to relieve distressed corporations.

Up to the time of his election, Franklin D. Roosevelt was also a believer in budget balancing, but as he prepared to assume the duties of office his ideas underwent a radical change, and his inaugural message was a call for prompt and vigorous action. During the first two terms of the Roosevelt Administration, numerous expedients were tried—monetary manipulation; "business self-government" under NRA codes; farm production controls; direct relief to needy individuals in cash and in kind; work relief projects administered directly by government agencies; public works spending on highways, bridges, schools, public housing, and so on; enactment of minimum wages and maximum hours; and establishment of the social security system. Throughout this period the approach was frankly experimental, the theoretical basis of policy was changed more than once, and recovery was far from complete when the war took over and finished the job.

Meanwhile a more systematic theoretical basis for government policy was being developed in the modern theory of employment.

The theoretical concepts have not changed particularly since the
end of the war, but great progress has been made in giving them
practical application by developing systems of national accounts
and other measurements of economic activity. Study of the labor
force and of labor market processes was rather neglected until a
few years ago but is currently very active.

The Second World War provided several years of sustained full
employment in the United States, as in most other countries. It
provided a striking demonstration of the potentialities of economic planning, although it required a degree of regimentation
we should not like to live with in peacetime. By the end of the
war, the conviction had taken hold throughout the industrialized
world that governments must assume responsibility for the level
of employment.

In the United States the Employment Act of 1946 emerged
from a rather bitter struggle between liberals and conservatives
in Congress. Although disappointing to the advocates of the original "Full Employment Bill," who wanted a stronger commitment
to the principle of compensatory spending, the act was nevertheless of great significance as a declaration of national policy.

The basic proposition was worded with unusual delicacy: "It
is the continuing policy and responsibility of the Federal Government to use all practical means consistent with its needs and
obligations and other essential considerations of national policy
. . . to coordinate and utilize all its plans, functions and resources
for the purpose of creating and maintaining . . . in a manner
calculated to foster and promote free competitive enterprise . . .
conditions under which there will be afforded useful employment
opportunities, including self-employment, for those able, willing
and seeking to work, and to promote maximum employment, production and purchasing power." The President was required to
submit an annual Economic Report which (among other things)
would define the levels of employment and the production and
purchasing power necessary to achieve the policy objectives, and
to set forth a program of legislation and administrative action.
Other new institutions included the Council of Economic Advisers
and the Joint Economic Committee.

Countries such as Great Britain also undertook formal responsibility for employment opportunity; and the Charter of the

United Nations, in Articles 55 and 56, included the following declaration.

Article 55.

With a view to the creation of conditions of stability and well-being which are necessary for peaceful and friendly relations among nations based on respect for the principle of equal rights and self determination of peoples the United Nations shall promote:

a. higher standards of living, full employment and conditions of economic and social progress and development;
b. solutions of international economic, social, health and related problems; and international cultural and educational co-operation; and
c. universal respect for, and observance of, human rights and fundamental freedoms for all without distinction as to race, sex, language and religion.

Article 56.

All members pledge themselves to take joint and separate action in co-operation with the Organization for the achievement of the purpose set forth in Article 55.

Problems of carrying out the commitment. In the first decade of the Employment Act, high employment was maintained in the United States except for moderate and relatively brief downswings in 1949 and 1954. Although there was some controversy concerning government policy during these recessions, the commitment to high employment was not really tested until after 1957. About that time, the immediate postwar era—which had been marked by frequent supply shortages, a persistent investment boom, and a favored American position in world markets—came to a close. Excess capacity developed, particularly in manufacturing and transportation industries. Profit margins narrowed. Labor markets as well as commodity markets became looser.

Since 1957 some of the great problems and complexities of carrying out the commitment to full employment have become apparent.

To begin with, it has been necessary to interpret the commitment. How much unemployment is consistent with the policy objectives? During the recent period of economic slack, there has been a tendency to relax the criteria. This tendency is illustrated by the Kennedy Administration's 4 per cent goal. Although it may be somewhat academic to debate whether 3 per cent or 4 per cent should be the goal, while the rate drifts along indefinitely at 6 per cent, still it is significant that the objective has been defined as a level of unemployment twice as high as the current level in many European countries.

Of course, the strength of the commitment has been diluted because it conflicts, or at least appears to conflict, with other desiderata. Even apart from the noninterventionist tradition, three principal constraints have affected the commitment.

First is the fear of inflation, held with an almost religious fervor in some quarters. There can be no doubt that in striking a balance between price stability and full employment, price stability has been favored to a much greater extent in the United States than in most other industrial nations. Between 1959 and 1962, for example, consumer prices rose 4 per cent in the United States as compared with increases ranging from 9 to 16 per cent in France, Germany, Italy, Japan, Sweden, and the United Kingdom.

Second is the balance-of-payments problem. In order to check capital flows, deflationary monetary policies have been pursued at the expense of economic growth. Whether these persistent deficits in long-term and short-term capital accounts actually require conservative monetary and fiscal policies is too complicated a question to be discussed here. A good argument can be made that domestic economic expansion will have a favorable effect on the balance of payments in the long run, but such an argument cannot be offered so confidently with respect to short-run impacts. In any case the exchange problem has given fiscal conservatives in the Treasury, the Federal Reserve System, and the financial community a strategic advantage which they would otherwise not have enjoyed.

The third constraint is the principle of the balanced budget, which is so deeply engrained in American thinking as to be almost an article of faith. How else can the virtual absence of grass-roots support for the proposed income tax cut in 1963 be explained? Actually the federal government account—whether in terms of budget receipts and expenditures or cash receipts and payments—has been unbalanced most of the time in recent years. Most European countries have had the same experiences, but they have suffered much less concern about the situation. But, while the federal debt has moved up slightly in the postwar period, GNP has more than doubled; so that the debt, which stood at 123 per cent of GNP in 1946, was only 55 per cent of GNP in 1962. Likewise there has been a substantial, although smaller, decline in the ratio between interest payments and the national income. Thus the real burden of the federal debt has been greatly reduced in the postwar period, but again it has been necessary to sacrifice an expansionary fiscal policy which would have been conducive to the attainment of employment goals.

The Kennedy Administration was, of course, aware of these constraints on employment policy and made various attempts to loosen them; but it cannot be said that the endeavor was very successful.

On various occasions the President and members of his Administration inveighed against primitive economic thinking and sought to instill greater sophistication with respect to fiscal policy. For a number of reasons the impact of the efforts was rather slight. The arguments were complex and difficult for laymen to understand; for example, the distinction between a "bad" federal deficit resulting from economic contraction and a "good" deficit designed to encourage expansion, through the medium of a low tax structure, was too subtle for most taxpayers even though it was really quite valid. Moreover, the arguments constituted a challenge to some deeply held traditional ideas. Finally, most of the Administration's utterances were couched in such impeccable orthodoxy as to nullify the effects of the occasional experiment in boldness.

The celebrated "Guideposts for Noninflationary Wage and Price Behavior," promulgated by the Council of Economic Advisers at the beginning of 1962, were an attempt to reconcile more closely the objectives of full employment and price stability. The Guideposts were not popular with either labor or management, and numerous questions of interpretation soon arose. By the end of 1962, after it had become apparent that unemployment, rather than inflation, was still the principal obstacle, the Guideposts had receded into the background. But the problem to which the Guideposts were directed is still potentially important. There is little reason to doubt that the price level would begin to climb once more if we should come close to full employment, and that a

cost push originating in administered-price industries would contribute to the trend. Most of the economically advanced countries
are struggling to find ways and means of encouraging noninflationary wage settlements without sacrificing the institutions of
free collective bargaining.

To improve the international balance of payments without reducing economic activity or antagonizing other friendly nations is
a difficult and delicate problem, to say the least. The Kennedy
Administration has tried a variety of expedients including "Buy
American" requirements, reduction of the tourist exemption, and
the "scissors" operation in which long-term interest rates are held
down to stimulate investment while short-term rates are kept up
to prevent the liquidation of short-term assets held by foreigners.
In 1963 President Kennedy proposed to tax interest from foreign
securities. In addition the United States has participated in co-
operative endeavors through the International Monetary Fund,
the Bank for International Settlements, and the Office for European Cooperation and Development, as well as various bilateral
arrangements, designed to support distressed currencies and provide adequate supplies of international reserve assets. Since none
of these measures has produced any decisive improvement, there
is reason to think that more basic changes in the international
monetary system will be necessary if the dollar is to remain an
international reserve currency while the United States continues
its foreign aid and foreign military programs.

Government policies for labor market adjustment. The Conference on Unemployment and the American Economy, which
led to this book, was concerned mainly with a critical evaluation
of federal government policies, most particularly the federal manpower program and fiscal policies. Although some speakers dealt
with such topics as anti-trust, hours of work, and minimum wages,
manpower and fiscal policies were the principal themes. But in a
predominantly private enterprise economy the policies of industry
and labor are also of great importance. In training and retraining,
for example, the federal government's program is only a drop in
the bucket compared with the vast amount of training conducted
by private corporations. The difference is that the government
trains the unemployed, whereas the corporations train employed

workers for higher positions. And private employment services make a larger number of placements in most labor markets than do the public employment operations. The role of collective bargaining should also be stressed. Job security and worker readjustment have been principal concerns of unions and employers during recent years, and numerous agreements have been negotiated covering supplemental unemployment compensation, termination pay, transfer rights for displaced workers, early retirement, shorter hours of work, and the like.[6]

The traditional role of the federal government in the labor market has been relatively modest except in time of war. Support has been given to vocational training and apprenticeship; minimum standards have been established for state unemployment insurance programs; activities of the state employment services are coordinated to some slight extent by the Bureau of Employment Security; information is collected and analyzed by the Bureau of Labor Statistics. But augmented concern over the need for better matching between labor supply and labor demand is reflected in three pieces of legislation enacted during the Kennedy Administration.

The first is the Area Redevelopment Act of 1961. As one element of a program for bringing new industry into distressed areas, training is provided to equip unemployed workers with new skills required by incoming industries or by other identifiable job vacancies in the area. Subsistence allowances roughly equivalent to unemployment insurance in amount are available for brief periods up to 16 weeks. As of July 1, 1963, a total of 440 projects, providing training for 21,715 unemployed workers at a cost to the federal government of $12,406,780, had been started.

The Manpower Training and Development Act embodies a more ambitious concept of retraining. Instruction is not limited to occupations which happen to be in demand where the unemployed workers reside, nor is the program restricted to distressed areas suffering unusually high unemployment rates. Training costs and subsistence expenses are defrayed for periods up to 52 weeks, rather than 16 weeks as under the Area Redevelopment Act. Furthermore, special projects are authorized for members of low-income farm families and for unemployed youth. As of April

30, 1963, over 1,000 projects had been approved and more than 40,000 unemployed persons had been trained, or accepted for training, in 247 different occupations.

The third new piece of legislation is the Trade Expansion Act of 1962. Assistance can be given to firms and to workers who are shown to be injured when tariff barriers are reduced or eliminated as a result of negotiations permitted by the act. Companies can be given technical, financial, and tax benefits; workers can receive "trade adjustment allowances" for periods of 52 weeks. Up to the present time, however, these provisions have not been activated.

Subsistence or adjustment allowances payable to workers under this new legislation are similar to unemployment insurance. Traditionally, however, unemployment insurance has been paid only to workers who remain in the labor market actively seeking jobs. Obviously a displaced worker cannot undertake a retraining course for six months or a year and be continuously available for work at the same time. Thus payments in the nature of unemployment insurance are being made to workers who, from a technical standpoint, are not unemployed because they are not currently looking for work. At the same time twenty states have amended their social security legislation to provide that unemployment insurance itself may be given to workers who enroll in approved training courses in order to improve their chances in today's labor market.

Here the beginning of a new concept of unemployment compensation can be discerned. The historic purpose has been to maintain the worker's income during brief spells of unemployment on the assumption that he would be recalled to his old job, or find a new one, within a few months. The new concept is a more ambitious one: that unemployment compensation (or some variant having a different name) can be used as a positive instrument of labor market adjustment, a means of assisting workers to conform to the new patterns of labor demand.

This concept of the augmented role of unemployment compensation in a positive labor market policy has been more intensively developed in Europe than in the United States. Relocation allowances, which have also been adopted in Europe, have been widely discussed in this country. In fact, the original draft of the Manpower Training and Development Act provided financial assistance for unemployed workers and their families who were willing to move into areas where they could more readily find jobs. Local interests in areas of high unemployment, who disliked the idea of losing population as a result of subsidized out-migration, opposed this feature; and it was stricken from the bill by the time of its ultimate passage.

Federal fiscal policy. Of all the federal policies affecting aggregate economic activity and employment, only the question of income tax reform is discussed at length in this volume.

Monetary policy is not dealt with to any great extent either, although a few of the authors do mention it incidentally. Likewise not much is said about government spending. If fiscal policy can be compared to scissors, spending is one blade and tax policy the other. During the 1930's expansionary fiscal policy was generally conceived in terms of public works and other types of augmented spending; in the 1960's there has been greater emphasis on reducing income taxes. But, although the Kennedy Administration did not publicly advocate higher spending for the purpose of stimulating employment, the fact is that expenditures have increased. Federal purchases of goods and services have risen from $55 billion in fiscal 1961 to an estimated $68 billion in fiscal 1964; total federal expenditures (on a national income accounts basis) have advanced from $98 billion to $119 billion. During this period social security tax rates have risen; and, although business firms have been offered more favorable depreciation allowances and tax credits for investment, up to the end of 1963 there had not been a general income tax reduction. Thus, although there has been more talk about taxes, actually there has been more movement in the area of spending.

The bulk of the increase in federal spending has been for defense and space, but in some quarters more spending for social improvement is urged. Speaking for the AFL-CIO on policies to restore full employment, Walter Reuther advocates "a major increase in public spending to meet our social deficits in such fields as education, health, housing, urban renewal, mass transportation and resource conservation and development, together with a substantial increase in international economic aid." [7] Although higher appropriations for defense and space have been obtained with little difficulty, Congress has resisted proposals for aid to education, mass rapid transit, and other social areas.

The discussions of tax policy involve a number of basic concepts. The case for a substantial tax reduction rests on the premise that the economy is suffering from chronically inadequate demand. In periods of economic recovery the rate of expansion tapers off before full employment is reached; and the gap between actual and potential GNP is widening as time goes on. One principal reason is the federal income tax structure, which was designed to deal with the strong inflationary pressures of wartime. As the Joint Economic Committee has stated,

. . . Taxes were adopted in an atmosphere of excess demand, of almost constant pressure on productive resources, and of excess liquidity sufficient to have generated a runaway inflation. With the passage of time federal tax policies have become outdated and ill adapted to present and prospective conditions.[8]

Under present conditions, tax revenues increase so rapidly as economic activity expands that the expansion is choked off before full employment is reached. The theory behind a tax cut is that lower rates will permit the expansion to continue until full employment has been approximated more closely. Since revenues depend on economic activity as well as on the structure of tax rates, a balanced budget can eventually be achieved at a higher level of activity.

This means that a budget deficit must be deliberately incurred until the tax cut has had time to make itself felt. Such a "planned deficit" is contrasted with the "passive deficit" characteristic of federal finance in recent years and resulting from a tax structure which represses private activity and therefore curtails the expansion of tax receipts.

To estimate the impact of a tax cut, the concept of the "tax multiplier" is used. Since consumers spend most of their tax savings, additional incomes are generated which in turn recirculate into the "spending stream." In addition to the consumption multiplier, it is anticipated that business firms will purchase more capital goods in order to meet the increased demand as consumer expenditures rise. This additional investment will have its own direct and indirect effects on employment. But, although consumer behavior is quite stable and predictable, investment behavior is not. For this reason estimates of the total effect of a tax reduction must be regarded as somewhat speculative.

In its 1963 report, the Council of Economic Advisers calculated that the total tax multiplier would be 3.5. This would mean that the $10 billion income tax reduction, proposed by the Kennedy Administration to take place in three stages, would eventually bring about a $35 billion increase in GNP. Dr. Heller discusses the tax multiplier at considerable length in Chapter 4. Although most economists support the validity of the Administration's general theory of a tax cut, the estimated multiplier of 3.5 seems highly optimistic. Has the Council "oversold" the tax cut?

NOTES

1. United States Department of Labor, *Manpower Report of the President,* March 1963, p. 40

2. President's Committee to Appraise Employment and Unemployment Statistics, *Measuring Employment and Unemployment,* 1963, p. 14.

3. United States Congress, Joint Economic Committee, *Hearings on the Economic Report of the President,* Part I, 1963, p. 439.

4. United States Department of Labor, Bureau of Labor Statistics, *The Extent and Nature of Frictional Unemployment,* Study paper No. 6 prepared for Joint Economic Committee, November 1959.

5. R. C. Wilcock and W. H. Franke, *Unwanted Workers* (Free Press of Glencoe, 1963), p. 11.

6. Some of the important actions taken by employers and unions to cope with unemployment and worker displacement will be discussed in forthcoming volumes of the Research Program on Unemployment and the American Economy. This book, however, is concerned largely with the manpower and fiscal policies of the federal government.

7. United States Congress, Joint Economic Committee, *Hearings on Economic Report of the President, op. cit.,* p. 654.

8. United States Congress, Joint Economic Committee, January 1963, *Economic Report of the President,* March 14, 1963, p. 3.

RETRAINING AND LABOR
MARKET POLICIES

CHAPTER 2

Next Steps in Labor Market Policy

BY WILLIAM HABER

The Centrality of Employment in a Job Economy

It is doubtful whether Americans as a nation have ever been as responsive to the employment levels and particularly the unemployment index as in recent years. The preoccupation shown with the problem is not limited to economists or practitioners involved in the administration of the pertinent state and federal programs. The political operators, in and out of office, are vitally concerned. Those on the outside know that the issue of jobs can win elections; and those in office recognize this fact too and are concerned lest the problem of joblessness become an important slogan of the opposition. We are not suggesting that the concern about the jobless is specious; quite the contrary, political administrations are deeply distressed about the problem. In a society in which a job represents the only source of livelihood and is also a social measure of worth and status, 4 to 5 million people who need work and want work cannot find it. No one can callously disregard such a tragedy of human frustration and waste.

31

Apart from these natural impulses possessed by men of good will, political realities do not allow for continued neglect or casual concern about unemployment and the unemployed and their families. Our sensitiveness to this waste is deep-seated. It goes back a full generation. The depression of the 1930's brought home to millions of Americans the full extent to which unemployment as a pathological problem can undermine the basic institutions of our society.

Out of that experience grew the Wagner-Peyser Act which established our federal-state employment services, the Social Security Act which led to the adoption of unemployment insurance legislation in all states, and the provisions of the Railway Labor Act which seeks to protect the job rights of railroad employees affected by mergers and consolidations. Out of the experience, although delayed by the intervention of the Second World War, came the Employment Act of 1946 which stressed the national interest in employment and the federal government's responsibility for taking necessary measures to maintain high levels of employment. Having established national concern and responsibility, it was inevitable that the federal government would step in with appropriate legislation whenever the federal-state system of unemployment insurance failed to accomplish its major mission, which is the payment of benefits to those involuntarily unemployed. Thus in 1958, during the Eisenhower Administration, Congress enacted a Temporary Unemployment Compensation Act for a two-year period to provide for those whose benefit rights were exhausted in the recession of that time.

And, again in 1961, the Kennedy Administration enacted another Temporary Emergency Unemployment Compensation Act for another two-year period to provide for those whose benefit rights under the state unemployment insurance laws were ended during the recession of 1960.

Nor is the more recent legislation, the Area Redevelopment Act of 1961 and the Manpower Development and Training Act of 1962, as well as the manpower features of the Trade Expansion Act of the same year, unrelated to this historical flow of events.

Employment and unemployment have become, in the minds of the public and of the political activists, the most sensitive indices of the nation's economic health, and it can be expected that, whenever the volume of joblessness for the nation as a whole suggests pathological manifestations, a host of legislative proposals will result and some legislative action—wise or not so wise—will follow.

Neglected Research Areas

Consequently, it becomes all the more important that our research on unemployment be expanded at all levels. If our concern in recent years has been with "class" rather than "mass" unemployment, research based on highly aggregated data and national income will not expose the more refined problems affecting particular regions or localities, and it will certainly neglect the particular categories which appear to be especially affected by the unemployment in the postwar recessions. This sort of unemployment, affecting significant segments of the labor force, calls for the labor market equivalent of microanalysis with which the economist is familiar. Such studies should be related to the behavior of the local labor market. Although a number of studies have been going on, we do not know enough, except in the most general terms, about local and regional labor markets, about labor mobility and the factors which aid or inhibit it, or about the effects of minimum wage laws, collectively bargained pensions, seniority provisions and the whole complex of "job rights" now being negotiated, and the general behavior of local, regional, and national labor markets. It is clear that we lack the methods of determining where job openings exist or are likely to develop. Surveys are time-consuming; the results are often unsatisfactory, and even employers cannot or will not formulate or divulge hiring plans. A search for new techniques is sorely needed.

Labor turnover, for example, declined substantially in recent years. Jobs are becoming "stabilized" for those who have them. Seniority rules provide substantial protection, except when work force reductions are really serious. And fringe benefits, including pension plans and vacation rights among others, often suggest that overtime at premium rates is financially more advantageous to the employer than the addition of new employees. The trend of building fences around the jobs for those who have them is bound to increase. Those who become redundant are to be transferred to a "labor pool"; no one is to be laid off; and it follows that, except under conditions of considerable expansion, few are to be hired in the established industries. This represents a forward step in increasing the job security of the presently employed labor force. When extended to major plans and industries across the land, it "fences in" those who work and makes more difficult the admission into such plants and industries of new entrants to the labor force. This development may be a natural one, and perhaps a desirable one. It begins to approach a job guarantee. It does, nevertheless, raise serious questions concerning opportunities for new workers.

We might take the position that our unemployment problem would quickly melt under the warm sun of a more vigorous rate of economic growth. Such a growth rate, one which would increase the gross national product by $30 or $40 billion, would soak up the pockets of unemployment and depress the unemployment rate to the more desirable level of 3 or 4 per cent of the labor force. Certainly, any increase in general levels of employment would simplify the problem of re-employment. It is now still serious in declining or depressed areas and in many other sections for certain categories of the labor force. However, recent observations of what has happened under improved economic conditions in many areas appear to suggest that this view is overly optimistic. A substantial amount of unemployment will continue even under a more vigorous prosperity than prevails at present. And to reduce it to acceptable levels requires more attention to the quality and direction of our manpower movement than we have normally provided.

Slow Development of Manpower Policy

That we shall need to know more and do more about our manpower is becoming increasingly clear. For a surprisingly large number of our important decisions have manpower implications —national, regional, state, and local. Yet we may not be quite ready for the development of a labor market manpower policy. A policy is based on a philosophy—an accepted point of view, an objective the majority seeks to obtain. I am not certain that we have a labor market philosophy, that we know what it is that we expect our programs to accomplish. For example, we are still discussing the objectives of unemployment insurance 25 years after we began the payment of benefits under that program. In the manpower area, the issues are more cloudy because they involve, for example, the relationship of the government to the economy, to the employer, and to the worker. Traditionally, the government has sought to provide basic education and, except for special wartime programs, a rather limited effort under the Smith-Hughes Act, some encouragement of apprenticeship training, it left occupational training to the local schools, to private institutions, and primarily to the workers and to the employer. "On-the-job" training has been the most common kind except for highly technical and professional occupations.

A labor market policy, however, is evolving; but it will come slowly, for it does involve a degree of interest and acceptance of responsibility by both national and local governments. And many will argue against diluting the employee's responsibility to find his own vocational niche.

Nevertheless, it is clear that the nation is increasingly involved in manpower policy. Much that we do in other areas has overwhelming manpower implications. We can cite, for example, the so-called "full employment policy" expressed in the Employment Act of 1946 and in the work of the Council of Economic Advisers; the proposals for federal aid to education, including vocational education, and especially in higher education; the proposal for a Youth Employment Opportunities Act with its provision for a youth conservation corps and for local area youth employment; the complex area of job discrimination and programs at national and state levels to reduce and eliminate it; and our serious preoccupation and concern with the quantity and quality of our scientific manpower.

More recently we recognized the manpower implications of our international trade policy and provided unprecedented protection by way of allowances and relocation costs to those who may be affected by trade agreements with other countries. These are not new problems; we are, however, beginning to recognize their relationships to the nation's manpower and its utilization. It is also significant to observe that most of these problems grow out of national policy decisions. Perhaps, without specifically intending to, we are beginning in a pragmatic way to create a national manpower program.

Human Consequences of "Creeping Unemployment"

Technological forces operating in our economy inevitably emphasize these developments. Little is to be gained by joining the debate as to whether the rate of technological change in the postwar period is substantially higher than that which prevailed in earlier decades. The statistical data are scant. It is sufficient to record, however, that the present changes in technology stimulated by a vital and growing "industry of discovery" (as the late Sumner Slichter called it) are taking place at a time when the national economy is growing at only a normal or less than normal rate and when the net increase in the labor force is considerably larger than in the preceding decade. Furthermore, these changes are occurring at a time when several basic industries are either reducing or not increasing their employment. The impact of technological change in railroad transportation, bituminous coal mining, textiles, and agricultural employment is constantly felt. The Secretary of Labor reports that the number of farm workers dropped from 7.4 million in 1950 to 4.9 million in 1962, a fantastic decline of 34 per cent in one decade. The displacement outlook in steel, rubber, autos, longshoring, and other industries in the years ahead suggests that we are truly in a period of major job adjustment for millions of workers. The consequent "withering away" of occupations will provide a major trial for millions of workers and a real test of educational, training, and placement services.

The recent and current excitement is not the result of these long-term developments. Our present concern grows out of a crisis of sorts, not very dramatic or catastrophic except for those who are directly affected. It has been referred to as "creeping unemployment" or as "unemployment during prosperity." It is not easy to determine whether this unemployment is due to a genuine weakening of demand or to structural factors. It is clear that unemployment rates in recent years have been considerably above those which prevailed in the immediate postwar period. Thus, while between 1947 and 1957 unemployment averaged about 4 per cent per year, it has equaled or exceeded 5 per cent of the labor force continually since 1957. It remained that high at the peak of the cycle in 1960 and has been higher in 1962 and 1963. A brief examination of unemployment rates in earlier periods indicates that these relatively high rates are exceptional; and that only during the period 1907–1912 and during the great depression of the 1930's was such a large proportion of the labor force out of work.

Perhaps equally significant is what has been referred to as the "upward drift" of the unemployment rates. Whatever the cause may be, recovery from each of the last three recessions appears to have left us with a higher rate of unemployment than the preceding recovery. If this trend persists, the next recession (and no one has yet written a prescription that protects us from one) is likely to end with 6 or 6½ per cent of the labor force out of work.

Of special significance is the fact that these high rates of unemployment have been associated with a higher volume of "long-term" unemployment than at any time since the end of the Second World War. In 1957, for example, 19 out of 100 jobless were out of work 15 weeks or more; in 1963, the figure was 28 out of 100. In January 1963, 1,153,000 workers were unemployed for 15 weeks or more; one-half of these were idle for 27 weeks or more.

In some of the major cities these long-term unemployed have become hardened into a class occupying the central city areas— an increasing number of persons who, as a recent issue of Business Week described them, "sift to the bottom of the economic heap during recessions and remain out of work during prosperous times." In large cities like Detroit a "hard core" not only exists but also persists as a "highly singular class of unemployed and unemployable socially and economically isolated from the rest of the economy." A California study suggests that unemployment has become almost a way of life for some groups—"forgotten segments of society, circles of depressed city dwellers caught by little education, low economic status, low employment opportunities and limited social contacts."

A Chicago report stated that no progress will result from the Manpower Development and Training Act or other devices unless drastic measures are taken to remove artificial social and economic barriers. Discrimination in housing concentrates all the unemployed in certain areas. Discrimination in hiring keeps whole neighborhoods on a poverty level. Such an environment fosters personality disturbances and antisocial behavior, repels the best-equipped teachers from its schools, and produces the increase of functional illiteracy which characterizes so many of our unemployed. Moreover, the parents in this group transmit to their children their own sense of hopelessness and defeat, perpetuating from one generation to the next conditions which make adaptation to jobs extremely difficult. So long as social and economic discrimination persists, programs like the MDTA can be of limited value only.

Persistent hard-core unemployment could easily be converted, as it no doubt already has been in many areas, to a high degree of unemployability immune to training, retraining, or jobs created by an economic boom.

A National Training Program—ARA and MDTA

These factors coupled with the increasing difficulties in finding jobs for the unskilled and the less educated led to the first adoption of a federally inspired and financed retraining program. The administration of the Area Redevelopment Act was provided with a small sum for retraining in depressed areas among its other authorizations for redevelopment grants and loans. The program was distinctly limited. Those to be trained had to be selected locally; the numbers were limited by the small appropriation; the period of training was confined to 16 weeks—but it was a beginning. Federal funds were provided to defray the cost of training and of allowances to the trainees. In a sense it was a fortunate beginning, for it provided some experience to guide the more ambitious MDTA which was adopted two years later.

In view of our limited experience in occupational training, MDTA could perhaps be referred to as a "crash program." It was assigned an ambitious undertaking for a two-year term with an appropriation of $265 million. An additional authorization of $165 million was provided for the third year to be expended on a matching basis with the states. Thus, if the states collaborated in full during the third year, there would be available a total of nearly $600 million for a three-year period. This is not a fabulous sum if it is judged by Congressional appropriations for high-priority programs. But, in view of the newness of the undertaking and the serious qualms entertained by many, it represented an expression of faith in an idea that can be justified only by the frustration with the problem of persistent hard-core unemployment.

The Manpower Development and Training Act was designed to meet the cost of training and to provide training allowances related to the amount of average unemployment insurance benefits, as well as subsistence allowances limited to $35 per week for those who must live away from home during the training period. The sums were to be apportioned among the states in relation to the labor force, unemployment and unemployment insurance coverage, and certain other considerations. It was estimated that about 560,000 persons might be trained during the three-year period; 100,000 the first year; 160,000 the second; and 300,000 the third year. Provision was made for the training of youth; allowances were limited, however, to those between 19 and 22 years of age and to $20 per week, with a further restriction that no more than 5 per cent of the total appropriation could be used for this purpose.

No one should underestimate the difficult task facing those responsible for administering a training program of this magnitude. There are job shortages now in many occupational groups, particularly in expanding areas. It is a challenging assignment to convert the unemployed: the short-term and the long-term, many displaced by technological changes in coal mines or industrial plants, most of them unskilled; many young workers with only brief attachment to the labor force; others in the upper-age brackets, thus difficult to retrain. Many of the unemployed have no occupational skills. Others have neither skills nor aptitudes that can readily be redesigned for the jobs available; this is especially true of older people.

The very characteristics of "class unemployment" suggest the complexities of any large-scale program for occupational retraining. The nonwhites, for example, represent 22 per cent of the unemployed and 24 per cent of those out of work for a period of 6 months or more. The unskilled and semiskilled represent 45 per cent of those out of work for more than 6 months.

The educational level of the group as a whole represents a most serious limitation and a striking warning as to what we should be doing about basic education if we are not to compound our problem in the future. The significance of the low educational level of the unemployed is suggested by the fact that a large proportion of those who were tested by the employment service before being referred for training failed to pass. The "hard core" may need more than a retraining program before they can be fully returned to productive employment. Individual, rather than mass, treatment by job placement services will be required for many.

Some observations about retraining: Prospects and limitations. It is not only risky but also somewhat inappropriate to appraise the effectiveness of the new retraining programs at this early date. The ARA has been in operation somewhat more than a year. The MDTA did not receive its appropriation until August 1962. The newness of the operation, coupled with competing administrative responsibilities both in Washington and in the states and localities, produced additional delays. Consequently, the program has been in effect less than a full year. One cannot generalize about so limited an experience. It is possible, however, to make some general observations about training and retraining without necessarily reflecting upon the operations of the MDTA. Several such observations suggest themselves.

Reason and reflection, rather than experience, suggest that we should deflate the exaggerated expectations of the retraining programs. That they are highly worthwhile is clear. And that training and retraining form an important part of any program to alleviate unemployment is equally clear. But, it seems, it would be a great error to regard these programs as a panacea, as a "solution," or even an important weapon against unemployment. Training and retraining are not a cure for unemployment; not even for the hard-core unemployed.

The number of people who can be retrained is also overstated. It is clear that the first year's results are likely to be considerably below the estimated number of 100,000. That is to be expected in view of the delay in the appropriation of funds, and other delays, not all of them inevitable.

We have unquestionably created a rather complicated administrative structure to deal with the problem. Several agencies are involved in the states and in Washington, and there are several even in the Department of Labor. When a training proposal is finally approved, after having gone through myriad hands, and having been the subject of hours or days of conferences, it is, as one observer put it, "like cracking peanuts with an anvil." Time and experience will resolve these administrative problems. Administrative difficulties are never by themselves a serious bar to the accomplishment of an important mission, once the significance of the mission is recognized. They do, however, represent distinct initial disadvantages and may explain in some part why the number who can be retrained in the early period will fall considerably below the forecast.

The program began with a great advantage. It started with the most obvious shortage occupations and with the most qualified workers among the unemployed. The ARA selection procedure appeared to favor younger workers; only 9 per cent of the males were over 44 years of age, although over 21 per cent of the unemployed are in that age bracket. The initial experience, therefore, may not be representative of the long-run problem.

The problem of the marginal worker has not yet been faced. During the second year the program will have to deal with those harder to train, less educated, older workers, who will barely pass the qualifying tests. There may, in fact, be considerable difficulty finding trainees with the qualifications that the schools estimate as a prerequisite for the training program. The truly hard core are likely to be bypassed.

Both the ARA and the MDTA programs have built-in limitations. ARA is clearly more limited since only redevelopment areas are eligible, and the maximum length of the training period is only 16 weeks. MDTA has other limitations, however. All training must be strictly job-oriented. This could be defined rigidly and, when it is so defined, a training course in reading and writing would be excluded. Such an interpretation would introduce a serious shortcoming because many of the unemployed cannot be placed on a job unless they have at least enough education to be functionally literate. A liberal interpretation, however, may permit the inclusion of such basic education by the clearly plausible reasoning that many, if not most, jobs require such literacy. The failure to allow such a flexible interpretation could be a substantial bar to the inclusion in retraining programs of those who need it the most.

An additional shortcoming is the limitation of training to 52 weeks. It is clearly insufficient to permit training of technicians. Their training may require considerably longer, in some instances even two years of college level education. Apart from technician training, however, there are many demanding occupations in which there are severe shortages which require more than the 52 weeks of training.

Youth unemployment a more serious problem. The limitation on youth employment is a serious error. Young people represent a disproportionate number among the unemployed. Their age, relatively low educational qualifications, and their inadequate job experience are likely to keep them unemployed a long time or to direct them to jobs without any hope of advancement. Many of them passed up the opportunity for basic education.

As of April 1963, the 5 per cent limitation led the Department of Labor to cut back sharply on the training allowances it has been paying the 19- to 21-year-old youth who do not qualify for regular federal training stipends. Payments to youth were running nearly 9 per cent of the total amount for training allowances, and in view of the Congressional restriction limiting these to 5 per cent, the cutback was inevitable. Such restriction does not apply to youth who are heads of families or have had three years' employment experience. The passage of the Youth Employment Opportunities Act would provide additional help in this significant and restricted area. Otherwise the limitations in the training act may bar many from an opportunity to learn now and thus complicate their occupational careers later.

The need for relocation allowances. It is difficult to determine to what extent the failure of Congress to include relocation allowances may in fact be a serious limitation. We know, of course, that such allowances are provided in several foreign plans, particularly in Sweden where as many as 10,000 allowances are made per year. The Swedish Labor Market Board thus encourages mobility from surplus areas to areas of labor shortage.

Would such travel allowances and, perhaps, additional grants be of substantial help in encouraging mobility in the United States? It is easy to come to an affirmative answer. The factors which discourage mobility are many and they are weighty. We have an exceptionally large number of wage earners who are also home owners. Even when not coupled with collectively bargained seniority rights and retirement pensions, home ownership may be a serious bar to mobility, especially when it involves the entire family. And, when proper weight is given to accrued "economic rights," pensions, seniority, and other accumulated rights in a particular plant, resistance to moving may be all the greater. Desirable and essential mobility is affected by a reluctance to leave home because of personal ties, because other members of the family may be working, by the cost of moving, and by possible home losses on local property and the insecurity in the new locality.

At the same time we should recognize that there still is much of the nomad in the American character. The record suggests that as many as 400,000 people may be working next month in some state other than the one they are in now.

This is not to suggest further research as a way of evading the proposal that relocation allowances should be provided. New industries are certainly developing and old ones vanishing at a greater speed than we realize.

Such allowances, when adopted, should be adequately circumscribed, but requiring a specific job with a definite employer and some assurance of continuity would represent too severe a restriction. One thing is clear: a program for relocation allowances calls for a vastly improved system of interstate job clearance and far greater reliance on the job information program of the public employment services than prevails today.

Vocational education: Modernization and Improvement imperative. The vocational education "image" in the American community has not been particularly attractive, except in a relatively few progressive states. Several state administrators involved in the MDTA operation have said that training continues in many moribund trades. One recent writer refers to these as "incredibly irrelevant to the facts of work in the 1960's." Training is often conducted in classrooms or shops with equipment hardly modern, to say the least, and often with teachers who are not intimately in touch with the skill requirements in their own community.

Responsibility for these shortcomings is diffused. The fact is that most Americans have given little status to vocational education. The vocational high school has often been looked upon as "the dumping ground" for those who cannot carry on in the academic courses.

Since it is, unfortunately, a fact that a substantial proportion of our young people do not continue beyond high school, the failure of our vocational training system results in inadequate preparation for "the working world."

The report of a Panel of Consultants on Vocational Education appointed by President Kennedy points out that vocational education now serves only 13 per cent of the 15- to 19-year age group of the nation. Even in large cities, which often have vocational high schools (and in some communities the most modern schools of the highest quality), only 18 per cent of those in grades ten through twelve are "exposed" to vocational training. Since about 20 per cent continue their education in colleges or universities, it appears that two out of three youths receive no real preparation for work before entering the labor force.

Perhaps two additional observations about vocational training are in order. The first is that the general criticisms of vocational training as it has been operated clearly do not apply everywhere. There are striking exceptions to the general weaknesses referred to in these remarks, such as the excellent vocational training institutions in communities such as Milwaukee and Cincinnati, among others.

The second has to do with the widely held view that vocational training itself is undesirable and unnecessary; that acquiring skills in the early ages is impossible; that occupations change too quickly; that those trained and retrained will have to be trained and retrained once more. In brief, the occupational revolution is proceeding too rapidly for anyone to be taught skills as if these were static.

What is called for, it is suggested, is broad general training not occupationally oriented. This goal is too ephemeral and not worth the investment of time and resources. Everyone committed to the "liberal arts" must concede the soundness of this point of view. Unfortunately, however, it is not universally applicable to the entire population, and our concern with vocational training is not for those who can absorb the basic elements of an academic education and who will do so. For these people, vocational education would be wasted. It is, however, a serious problem for those who "cannot make the grade"; and "learning to work" at some skill is far superior to no preparation at all.

Since MDTA training courses are to be carried on under the direction of the vocational educational system, in its classes and with its teachers, these shortcomings in vocational education represent both a danger and an opportunity. The danger is that the limitations of our vocational education program may well be a serious obstacle to the effectiveness of new training. "Bottlenecks" have already appeared. And, if this situation can arise when less than 40,000 trainees are involved, it can become quite serious when the numbers increase, even if the estimates are optimistic.

At the same time the very existence of MDTA may revitalize the entire vocational training system, modernize it, infuse some status into it, and provide funds for many new teachers, up-to-date equipment, and more financial support on a continuing basis. All are important. The Panel of Consultants referred to above recommends many changes in line with developing occupational requirements and the infusion of additional funds, a total of $400 million of annual federal grants for vocational education. It will take time to bring about the drastic changes necessary in vocational education. The system has already had a long history and strong "self-interest groups," many of whom fear change.

Training allowances: The place of unemployment insurance. Payment of allowances to those in training represents a great forward step. Without such payment the training program would never have gotten underway on a mass basis. How to assure the continuance of such payments when the legislation expires is worth exploring. It would be highly desirable if, as a consequence of the MDTA, the state unemployment insurance laws would permit eligible wage earners to receive insurance benefits while in attendance at approved courses. Until recently in only two jurisdictions was it possible to pay such benefits to employees enrolled in training programs. Even in these jurisdictions, the provisions were largely neglected. In Michigan, for example, over $300 million was paid in unemployment insurance benefits in 1958. But a very small number of trainees—less than 100—were actually paid while enrolled in a training program. The requirements—that the unemployed worker be "available for work" and be "actively seeking work" and that he be disqualified when he fails to accept a suitable job or respond to a recall notice from his last employer—all conspire to deny him a weekly benefit when his unavailability is due to participation in a retraining course. Such legislation is penny-wise and, in my judgment, represents a strong indictment of the state unemployment insurance systems. Such restrictions were partly inspired by the experience-rating provisions in our state legislation, but also by the failure to see unemployment insurance as part of a comprehensive labor market program. The employer to be "charged" with the benefit did not wish to have the cost of allowance charged to his account, since the employee was in fact not available for work.

This situation is changing rapidly. Twenty states have now revised their state legislation to make it possible for unemployed wage earners in attendance at approved training courses to receive the unemployment insurance benefit to which they are entitled. Many of these laws are still quite restrictive. It is hoped that more states will enact such authorization. There is a strong case for a federal standard in this area, and a requirement under which the state cannot deny weekly benefits to an otherwise eligible claimant who is undergoing retraining would provide allowances on a continuing basis should the federal legislation fail to be renewed. It is clear, of course, that during the life of the MDTA the trainee is not eligible to receive both the federal allowance and the state unemployment insurance benefits.

There is no reason why state unemployment insurance funds should not also be used to pay tuition and other costs of occupational training when and if the federal legislation expires. It could easily be arranged that such costs would not be charged to the last employer but should be borne by all employers covered by the unemployment insurance plan.

Early placement record encouraging. Whatever shortcomings of retraining may be cited, there should be no doubt that the development is highly desirable. There are few areas of government expenditures where the returns are likely to be higher. The very presence of the program has provided real hope for thousands of people; and next year, perhaps, to more than a hundred thousand. Many "graduates" have obtained jobs without the intervention of the employment services; others have been recruited by employers before the completion of their courses. The findings of

Gerald Somers' studies are fully supported by several state directors. They show that many workers who had months and even years of unemployment prior to retraining were placed on jobs shortly after completing their course. The Director in Michigan advised that 80 per cent of the people who had completed their courses under ARA or MDTA and who had been placed "would not have had jobs if it had not been for the training received." The placement record is not perfect; many have not been placed. One cannot say, however, that the investment was not worthwhile even when a placement failed to materialize. It is doubtful whether placement alone should be the criterion for judging the value of the training program. That it is an important measure and in the public mind the only one is, of course, quite clear. There are, however, intangible aspects of training which should not be overlooked. The mere fact of public interest in the problem of joblessness is an important morale booster; it has restored self-confidence and increased individual enterprise in job seeking, often with success in spite of earlier failure.

Extended duration of unemployment benefits important. It would be naive, indeed, to expect that a training and retraining program would represent a practical solution for the jobless problem for all, or even most, of the long-term unemployed. Shortage occupations in general require the sort of aptitudes and educational background which an overwhelming proportion of the jobless wage earners do not possess. That is certainly true for those who are out of work now. Quite apart from the educational limitations and skill potential of the jobless, present and future, the unemployment insurance program which has been developed in this country since 1936 is generally expected to meet the immediate problem for a vast majority of the unemployed. Our experience with postwar recessions suggests that our jobless insurance system, with its present limitations in the duration of benefit payments, has not been adequate to meet the problem. Its failure in this respect was recognized in 1958 when Congress enacted the TUC plan extending benefits for an additional period up to 13 weeks in states which passed appropriate legislation. This action was taken again during the recession of 1960; this time the Federal TEUC was so designed that it applied to all states. Both measures were of an emergency character and temporary. They have since expired. Barring a substantial liberalization in the duration provisions of the 51 unemployment insurance laws, it can be predicted that the next recession will again find a substantial proportion of the unemployed exhausting their benefit rights under the state legislation.

Retraining programs are most inappropriate for this sort of extended unemployment. So are programs of either the public works or the work relief variety. They are too costly and not sufficiently diversified to provide useful employment for more than a small proportion of the unemployed. Our experience suggests that long-range planning for such projects, while attractive in theory, is most difficult in practice. Political and technical obstacles result in long delays, often until after the employment crisis has begun to ease.

The unemployment insurance program was designed to meet the needs of the unemployed expeditiously. It sorely needs improvement in several respects, but especially so as to make unnecessary another TUC or TEUC. Our measures should not be temporary nor handled as emergencies. We have enough experience to anticipate these problems. And we know for certain that our action in 1958 and 1961 will have to be repeated, if not in 1964, then in 1965, or a year later. The case for a permanent extended benefit program is unassailable. And it is unfortunate that such action is not likely to be taken by the present Congress, at least not this year.

There appears to be substantial agreement that such extended benefits are necessary and desirable. There are, however, strong differences about how best to achieve this result. Should the extension of benefits beyond the present duration of 26 weeks prevailing under most laws be left exclusively to the states; or should it not be required as a federal standard; or enacted by Congress as a permanent national supplementary program? The case for making it applicable to all states is stronger. National concern about provision for the unemployed is being increasingly recognized. Such responsibility cannot be shirked, and direct federal legislation, or a federal standard for state legislation, is in order. Either will accomplish the objective of extended benefits for involuntary unemployment wherever it exists and whenever such payments are needed.

More controversial is the question whether such benefits should be financed by the employer, by the employee, or out of general revenues. These are not simple issues.

Until we adopt a general public assistance program to deal with need created by unemployment, it is inevitable that in any crisis we shall look to the unemployment insurance schemes as the logical and simplest way of dealing with the problem. This will impose burdens which the schemes were not intended to carry; it will add to the cost and often will seriously complicate the "insurance character." There is a strong case for extending the public assistance features of the Social Security Act to include, as an additional category, aiding need resulting from unemployment.

Basic education a serious weakness. Even a cursory examination of the characteristics of the unemployed highlights the sad state of educational affairs. The gaps in basic education are overwhelming. It may be possible to teach people who are illiterate in arithmetic the fundamentals so that they can fill out orders or read instructions. And courses with ARA and MDTA should permit such instruction, if there are serious questions about it. The larger problem remains, however. Many who formerly were most vocal in their support of vocational training now recognize the importance of basic education. The relationship between courses in basic education and the individual's employability is not always clearly evident. Not all subjects in high school, for example, would increase a youth's job-getting possibilities. The lack of such basic education, beyond functional literacy, may be a real bar to employment and certainly to progress in employment. We need to insist on a program of basic education for all our citizens; we need to conquer illiteracy without delay. Poorer countries who value education and human worth less than we do have accomplished it. It is shameful that such elementary ignorance should prevail and become a bar to employment for tens of thousands. Basic education should be a part of our national policy, and it should be broader in scope than would be required if related only to labor market policy. To be sure, the labor force would profit from basic education. But such labor force advantages should be incidental. Anyone who is below the standard of literacy should have an opportunity to become literate.

We should not overlook the fact that in some occupational areas labor shortages may be related to wages and working conditions. This is said to be true for registered and practical nursing. Adequate wages in hospitals and clinics would attract more trainees for these essential occupations. It is an important caution to those responsible to be aware that training more nurses is likely to depress wages further and lead many already registered and capable to leave this work. Training alone will not meet the existing shortage.

We must be careful lest large-scale nation-wide programs to retrain the unemployed impede the development of local programs. Such programs exist in a few states and in several cities. Local efforts can often be more carefully designed and related to existing job opportunities in the community.

It is equally important to avoid any development which may decrease the ongoing "on-the-job" training programs in our businesses and industries. Except for professional jobs and certain highly skilled crafts, most American workers are trained on the job. Much of the work in an assembly plant is individualized, related to the specific requirements of a company wherein the work is performed. It is an informal sort of training at the company expense. The MDTA recognizes these programs, and authorization for on-the-job training is recognized in the legislation. Steps to implement this phase of the work have recently been taken. Such a relationship between the training agency and the employer has many potential advantages.

The role of the employment services. The effectiveness of a retraining program depends on whether there will be jobs for those who are retrained; it depends also on the competence of the educational structure to which the retraining task is assigned; and to a considerable extent on employment service. Without an efficient and widely accepted local, state, and federal system offering a variety of employment services, the entire program can fail. However, the employment service has a vital role in community labor market management quite apart from the relationship to training. Its information-gathering function is vital. Its success depends largely on the relationships it is able to establish with employers in the locality. In the absence of sanctions, and these are available only in times of war or similar emergency, the service must find acceptance by employers and employees; it will be judged by the efficiency and quality of its performance.

It is not particularly disturbing that "national penetration rate" of the employment service (based on average monthly new hires in 1960) is only 15 per cent; nor that it varies from a low of 6 per cent for mining, 8 per cent for skilled workers, 10 per cent for professional and managerial, and 21 per cent in manufacturing; nor that only in placing the unskilled does it participate in as much as 30 per cent of the placements. Experience in Britain and on the continent is not substantially better.

Most American wage earners prefer to find their own jobs, to rely on tips from friends and relatives, and to shop around at various company employment offices. There would be many advantages if a larger proportion of the job seekers were "processed" through a public employment service. Such a development cannot be forced. It would be unwise to require employers to list all their vacancies with a public employment office. It has been suggested that such requirement should be made a condition for the right to participate in the experience-rating features of the state unemployment insurance law. There are ample justifications for such a course in times of national emergency, but its necessity in normal times may be doubted. Whether such a flow of new "business" would materially improve the role of the local or state employment office is likewise doubtful.

The employment office must "make its way" in the community of management and labor; its services must be valued and useful to all classes of wage earners. This situation prevails in many communities where diversified services exist. In some areas the local office is "involved" with the school authorities in planning the vocational curriculum; with employers in estimating the labor demand and supply outlook; with employees in counseling, testing, job referral, and placement; with other states in interstate clearance of job openings. Much depends on the imagination of the staff and the historical relationships which have been established between the employment office and the local employing institutions.

In some communities the local employment office is, in fact, a central local labor market agency, with accurate information because of ample contacts with employers and labor, and free of the old stigma that it is "merely a central station for the payment" of unemployment insurance.

Such is not the fact, however, in most U.S. communities. It will take much effort before most of the 1,900 local employment offices achieve such a position of acceptance and recognition. The work imposed on the office by the MDTA should further invigorate the employment services. Testing, counseling, job referral, placement, interstate job clearance for skilled as well as for other workers, must become services of such quality that the entire economic community will value them. That is not the case today.

That the employment service has continued to improve and to make an important contribution in "the organization of the labor market" is clearly evident to many. At the same time it is equally clear that it has not won wide acceptance in the economic community. This is not the place to review the reasons for its failure in this respect. Many reasons explain the "fixation" in the mind of the employer and the employee as to the appropriate function of the employment service. It is sufficient to recognize that, until these fixations are overcome, the employment service will have difficulties in becoming the community's central manpower planning agency.

And such an agency it must become. It needs to expand rapidly and aggressively in placement in skilled occupations, and in its role in the white-collar, technical, semiprofessional, and professional areas. This task is not easy. Private fee-charging agencies are bound to resist any encroachment, and employers are not likely to come to the support of the public employment service now or in the near future. Appreciation for the role of the public employment service will only develop with greater understanding and respect for manpower as a vital and limiting factor in our economic progress.

A National Manpower Program

The country sorely needs a national manpower program. Bits and pieces of such a program are strewn over the economic landscape. The heart of such a program must be full employment, however it is defined. Unless more jobs are developed, all other measures are palliatives which evade and avoid the only solution to unemployment consistent with a job economy. We also need a labor market policy on a continuing basis. Too much of what we do had its origin during the great depression or has been created in response to an emergency. Our manpower resources cannot be neglected: millions left without adequate basic education; many ill equipped for the occupational requirements of these times and without proper counseling and direction. Perhaps, out of the present investigation into why we have critical unemployment during prosperity, we may begin necessary steps toward the creation of a national manpower program.

Congress appears to have recognized these developments, and Title I of the MDTA is called "Manpower Requirements, Development, and Utilization." Congress recognizes the increasing centrality of the manpower role in the American economy and, to quote from Sec. 101 of the legislation, "that improved planning and expanded efforts will be required to assure that men, women and young people will be trained and available to meet shifting employment needs." And, moreover, "that it is in the national interest that the opportunity to acquire new skills be afforded" to those whose skills may become obsolete because of occupational and other technical changes. And, consequently, "It is therefore the purpose of this Act to require the Federal Government to appraise the manpower requirements and resources of the Nation, and to develop and apply the information and methods needed to deal with the problems of unemployment resulting from automation and technological changes and other types of persistent unemployment."

CHAPTER 3

The First Year of the Manpower Act

BY SEYMOUR L. WOLFBEIN

Economic Growth and Labor Market Policy

What is full employment? The common consensus regarding
the current employment and unemployment situation in the
United States is that we need, on the one hand, simultaneous and
interacting policies and programs which will stimulate economic
growth and, on the other, an active labor market policy.

It is widely recognized that a step-up in the rate of economic
growth is basic to the desired reduction in unemployment, the
rise in living standards we wish to generate, the momentum in
activity we have subscribed to internationally. It is also widely
recognized that all this will not occur if we do not follow policies
and carry out programs which anticipate wide differentials in
employment and unemployment among industries, occupations,
geographic areas, and population groups: policies which strike at
the rigidities and impediments to a responsive labor market, and
which ameliorate the deficiencies in the education and training of
the current and prospective labor force.

54

A high rate of economic growth is neither a necessary nor a sufficient condition for full employment. A theoretical model demonstrating this fact is easy enough to construct (for example, under conditions of relatively slow labor force growth, little technological change); the empirical evidence from a real-life situation is easy enough to adduce by reference, for example, to the experience in Great Britain during the postwar period.

Of course, in our own current situation, with a demographic base for very substantial labor force growth and with significant technological change taking place and looming ahead, higher rates of economic growth than we have achieved in recent years are absolutely essential. Furthermore, the prognosis for successful labor market policies is significantly enhanced by such economic growth.

But rapid growth by itself may fall short of gaining full employment (with sharp growth in labor force and technological change); the high rates of growth in some states still troubled by high unemployment are in point. If the composition of growth is heavy in sectors requiring little expansion in employment to yield greater output, positive employment effects will be limited.

In addition, an active labor market policy is a necessary, but not sufficient, condition for full employment. Except for a completely static situation, I have not been able to construct a realistic model which supports full employment without the inclusion of important elements of an active labor market policy; neither have I been able to find empirical evidence for the same. In fact, one of the striking features of postwar experience in Great Britain is their more effective labor market management, with a more comprehensive national employment service than ours, a youth employment service, vastly larger vocational education and apprentice training programs, and the like. Incidentally, the sheer geographic size and the cultural and income variations in different parts of this country intensify the significance of labor market policy in the United States.

An affirmation of propositions such as those just cited raises the urgent question of what definition of full employment is used. There is quite solid agreement on a theoretical formulation of full employment, especially when it is simply put in terms of optimum utilization of available manpower resources, with room left for some minimal unemployment rate below which it is hard to get, even with a very active labor market policy. Disagreements begin to emerge when the theoretical definition is then translated into some quantitative goal. As we all know, there has been considerable discussion of the quantitative sights we should set for ourselves.

But the heart of the problem really lies in the very fact that both theoretical and practical goals are ordinarily formulated by reference only to an aggregative level of unemployment and without reference to the disaggregative approach. What our two propositions are based on—and what would make a definition of full employment much more meaningful—is the definition of full employment in terms of (a) the desired overall employment of our manpower resources and a corresponding minimum overall rate of unemployment, and (b) the desired utilization of our manpower resources by age, sex, color, geography, industry, occupation, and so on, and a correspondingly minimum set of differential unemployment rates. Is a 2 or 3 per cent overall unemployment rate (but with 6 or 7 per cent unemployment for nonwhites or in any major occupational grouping) completely satisfactory "full employment"? Only when we have made an effective and lasting reduction in the almost classic differentials in unemployment will we be able to say we have achieved "full employment." A significant amount of active labor market policy will be required.

At this stage of the game, the point is often made that a high enough rate of economic growth—aided by labor market policies which can bring a low enough employment rate even lower without the danger of inflation—will do all of this for us. The evidence to substantiate this point is lacking; the only periods during the past quarter of a century when a reasonable facsimile of full employment was reached were during the years of the Second World War and the Korean War and their immediate aftermaths; and these were periods of most active labor market policy indeed.

The fact is that the abnormally high unemployment rates among certain sectors of our population do represent a ranking problem. The rate of unemployment among professional and technical workers has not gone above about 2 per cent, on an average annual basis, at any time during the entire postwar period. Indeed, the unemployment rate of any of the white-collar groups (professional, managerial, sales, and clerical), on an average annual basis, has rarely been above 4 per cent throughout the postwar period. (The rate for the sales group was 4.6 per cent in 1961; 4.1 per cent in 1962.) Of the eleven major occupational groups for which unemployment rates are regularly published, only three show rates above the national average: semiskilled operatives, service workers (excepting household service), and unskilled laborers. The last group's rate has usually been about double the national average. Nonwhites have consistently had a rate double the national average. We are now in the tenth consecutive year in which the unemployment rate for youths 16–19 has been running close to triple the national average. During this time, their rate of joblessness has never been below about 10 per cent and is now running at about 15 per cent.

As we all know, these examples can be extended by reference to other groups, but they suffice to indicate that such differentials do exist, that they are sharp, and that they have persisted over long periods—in good times and in bad.

An active labor market policy. If one agrees that the objectives of a labor market policy can be defined as achieving and maintaining, in conjunction with monetary, fiscal, and other measures, a full employment level of activity as we have defined it, then such a policy would include at least the following elements.

1. An up-to-date current labor market information service for workers and employers, to assess and communicate the results of such information as job vacancies, occupational needs, availability of workers and skills wherever this type of information counts.

2. An early warning system to communicate impending changes where they count, for example through the employment services, so that preventive measures can be immediately initiated to place in jobs or in training those who are scheduled to be displaced; similarly, early warning of expansion would facilitate efficient manning and growth.

3. An effective informational service for career guidance and counseling beginning at the elementary school level and continuing throughout a person's working life.

4. An educational system, vocational as well as academic, which is responsive to current and upcoming manpower needs.

5. A well-endowed system of placement services which focuses not only on a local labor market but nationally as well.

6. A program of training and retraining for unemployed and underemployed workers, as well as a program for equipping employed skilled workers with additional skills to meet increasing technical demands.

7. A program facilitating the mobility of workers which is responsive to the changing geography of employment opportunities.

Government will play an important role in implementing these programs at federal, state, and local levels; but labor and management also must assume increasing responsibility for each of them. As Secretary of Labor Wirtz has indicated, the "manpower" aspects of the industrial relations scene are becoming much more central in current discussions. While wages and working conditions continue, of course, to be vital, the really intractable emergent problems are concerned with adjustments to marked changes in technology, as was evident in the recent eastern longshoremen's strike, the newspaper strike in New York, and the railroad disputes.

There are other programs which usually are not included in listings of elements of an active labor market policy, but which definitely belong there. There is, first, a set of programs which plays a vital role in making for a better match between job opportunities and the people available to fill them. These range from antidiscrimination policies (by race, age, sex, and so on), to the provision of adequate housing and community facilities, to child-care centers.

Second, there is a set of income-sustaining measures such as unemployment compensation and public assistance which underlines the intimate relationship between labor market policies and programs for economic growth. Unemployment insurance is a particular case in point, in that it serves to sustain income and spending on the one hand, while maintaining the unemployed during the interval between jobs on the other.

Relation of labor market policy to economic growth. No discussion, even one as brief as this, can omit at least some reference to the contributions of labor market policy to economic growth. In this conference, which has a major interest in potential avenues of research, particular attention should be paid to this matter. It is, for example, one specific area marked for increased research in the Manpower Committee of the OECD.

In this connection, let us consider the following seven points.

1. Matching and filling job vacancies with unemployed men and women, for example, through training and retraining, makes an obvious contribution to economic growth. It is, in fact, an axiom of our trade that the total number of job vacancies represents the major contribution which a training and retraining program can make to economic growth. Unemployment, associated with zero production and zero earnings, can be converted by retraining and associated labor market programs to employment, production earnings, tax payments, and the like.

2. At the same time, the multiplier effects of this action can be considerable. The first is generated by the impact of a shift from unemployment to employment. The second is generated by the fact that the filling of a job often calls for the filling of associated jobs with additional multiplier effects. In a given field, the filling of job vacancies among professional staff would call for corollary hiring of secretarial and clerical assistance. Experience has also shown that the filling of auto mechanic vacancies requires hiring of auto mechanic helpers. When nurses are hired, nurses aides must be recruited.

3. As Professor R. A. Gordon, who chaired the recent President's Committee to Appraise Employment and Unemployment Statistics, can attest, job vacancies represent a peculiar statistical problem indeed. What makes data collection so difficult is that job vacancies come to life (and to light) when the right kind of person shows up. We have no idea, of course, how many of these job vacancies are kindled into reality when qualified personnel are supplied at the right time and right place, but that there are many seems certain in light of our past experimenting with this kind of enumeration.

4. In purely economic terms, labor market policy can also be viewed as part of a program for making investment more attractive by reducing the marginal cost of labor. In its own way, it is analogous to programs for making reductions in the price of capital through cuts in the interest rate or through more liberal

depreciation allowances. For example, training programs make available to employers trained workers when they need them and where they need them, especially since the advent of the Manpower Development and Training Act of 1962 which requires that training programs be carried out where job needs are documented. Thus, with a moderate increase in demand, employers who might otherwise hesitate to expand production have a better prognosis for getting the labor they need. Moreover, for many employers, training their own labor force may be impossible because of limited production activity, lack of facilities, or other factors. In this way, especially in conditions of less than full employment, labor market programs, including training, can be viewed as part of a comprehensive set of activities to stimulate economic growth.

5. Labor market activities involve substantial investments in plant and equipment with growth-generating potentialities like any other investments; personnel needs are also created for instructors and allied workers. At current rates the training operations under both the Manpower Development and Training Act and the Area Redevelopment Act are costing about $1,000 per worker being trained. About 40 per cent is going for training costs (equipment, salaries, and so on) and 60 per cent for training allowances. The $1,000 figure is gross cost, of course; most of those being trained would be receiving unemployment insurance for at least some of the interval involved.

6. Investment in education and training results in a labor force endowed with the skills and talents which the economy needs to encourage economic growth. They are just as necessary as the right kind of capital equipment and entrepreneurial skill.

7. The potentialities of training and retraining can also be seen from our accumulating evidence that it is possible to improve wages and working conditions through the training process itself. For example, we already have several instances in the relatively low-paying health service occupations where hospital administrators have agreed to a higher entry wage for workers with a background of training.

Beyond the values for economic growth and improved productivity, there are, of course, incalculable social values in achieving higher-quality employment, and in better suiting of jobs to workers' abilities and interests.

Training and Retraining

An active labor market policy and programs of training and retraining do not constitute a new dimension of social and economic life. There are significant references to the subject in the basic Judeo-Christian writings right up to Pope John XXIII's *Mater et Magistra*, with its important allusions to including training those affected by technological change.* The same, of course, can be said of the literature in the field of economics, from its earliest beginnings through the classical theorists to current writers.

In our own history, aside from the general field of education, we have had some good examples of an active labor market policy in the Homestead Act of a century ago, a very interesting example of government action stimulating mobility in manning a new frontier; in the immigration laws which saw, in the first decade of this century, a million persons a year enter this country to help us man a burgeoning industrial sector; and just the opposite policy right after the First World War—at which point emerged substantial government support of apprenticeship training programs as the supply of craftsmen from abroad was cut off.

Therefore our current programs of training and retraining have had a significant and mostly honorable evolution; they depend substantially for their implementation on ongoing institutional arrangements. What makes them new, of course, is their design and their legislative and administrative formulation to meet current problems. But they are part and parcel of our continuing problem of making a more perfect match between the individual and his environment—in this case, that part of his environment we call the world of work.

Early results. A substantial amount of statistical information relating to the characteristics of training programs and trainees has become available, and much more will be forthcoming as reporting systems become operational. In this discussion only a few

---

* See, especially, paragraphs 94, 95, and 96 of *Mater et Magistra*, Encyclical Letter of His Holiness Pope John XXIII on Christianity and Social Progress, May 15, 1961.

summary tables will be presented; additional data are available from our Office of Manpower, Automation and Training.* It must be emphasized, however, that the program is at its genesis, and the data should be used with some care since the numbers involved in many tabulations are still relatively small.

To date, the following points warrant mention in an evaluation of the training and retraining programs thus far.

1. President Kennedy signed the Manpower Development and Training Act (MDTA) on March 15, 1962; appropriations became available on August 14, 1962; contracts with the states began to be signed soon afterward. In the seven months or so since then, training projects covering about 33,000 trainees have been approved in every state except Louisiana, and in the other jurisdictions eligible under the act (Puerto Rico, District of Columbia, Virgin Islands). Currently about 2,000 persons a week are being approved for training, a figure approximating the schedule for this fiscal year.

2. A little over 1,000 different training projects, to which the 33,000 persons have been committed, are involved. This item deserves emphasis in view of the fact that each project requires an assessment of what jobs are available in the community for which training can be given (the law requires there be a reasonable prognosis for getting a job after training); the guidance, counseling, testing, and selection of eligible persons; the development of the required curricula and training sites; and the acquisition of needed equipment and teaching personnel.

3. If the program continues at its present momentum, between 60,000 and 70,000 persons will be approved for training during the current fiscal year. If appropriations are made available, another 140,000 may be approved during the next fiscal year. These numbers are cited so that they can be juxtaposed against the 4 to 5 million unemployed we have had in recent times. They emphasize the fact that the training effort is small, experimental, and only one part of an overall labor market policy.

* A current periodical entitled *Training Facts* brings together this kind of information and is available upon request from OMAT, U. S. Department of Labor, Washington 25, D.C.

4. As the program unfolds, the number of job vacancies which can be used to document the need for training is impressive. For example, under the ARA, where we are limited, by definition, to areas of substantial and persistent unemployment, enough job vacancies exist to put into training all the people we can with the funds available. With an unemployment rate between 5½ and 6 per cent since MDTA got under way, documenting jobs to support training programs has not been a limiting factor in the program.

5. More than 150 different occupational fields have been represented so far in approved training programs. The act carries no limitation on the kinds of jobs for which training can be conducted, with the exception of those which would require less than two weeks of training. The result has been a very wide spectrum of job fields, as can be partly seen from the summary in Table 1 which covers the first 31,000 trainees.

6. Some of the highlights of Table 1 warrant separate comment. Thus almost one out of every ten is being trained for a professional or managerial job. Most are training for medical service occupations (licensed and practical nurses, lab assistants, operating room technicians) and draftsmen, but the range is actually quite wide and includes programmers, statistical quality control assistants, and engineering aides.

More than one in five trainees are being prepared for clerical and sales jobs. In very large part, these are women learning secretarial, stenographic, and typing skills. Included are bilingual, legal, and medical secretaries. The group also includes bookkeepers, accounting clerks, key punch operators.

The largest group of trainees, one-third of the total so far, is aiming at skilled industrial jobs. These, of course, are mostly men, unlike the clerical group. Many are being trained for entry level jobs in the crafts as well as in pre-apprenticeship courses; but a significant number, especially in the repair occupations, are being brought up to date, building on skills they already have acquired in previous training and in their work experience. The large number being trained for repair occupations, where shortages of qualified personnel do exist, is particularly impressive.

7. It should be noted (Table 1) that a significant number of trainees are in courses leading to semiskilled jobs, mostly as general machine operators in metalworking. This point is mentioned

TABLE 1. Occupational Distribution of Approved Products
under MDTA—First 31,000 Trainees

Total	*100.0%*
Professional and Managerial	8.9
Medical service	5.0
Draftsmen	2.0
Other	1.9
Clerical and Sales	22.5
Secretaries	1.7
Stenographers	9.0
Typists	7.7
Salespersons	2.3
Other	1.8
Skilled	32.2
Metalworking machinery craftsmen	10.8
Auto mechanics and repairmen	8.8
Other mechanics and repairmen	5.7
Construction craftsmen (entry)	2.7
Woodworking machinery (entry)	1.3
Other	2.9
Semiskilled	26.7
Metalworking machinery operators	14.2
Textile machinery operators	4.0
Electronics assemblers	2.4
Leather, leather products workers	1.4
Other	4.7
Service	8.6
Medical service aides	4.0
Waiters, waitresses	1.8
Cooks	1.6
Other	1.2
Agriculture	*1.1*

separately because it is often observed that impending changes can upend some occupations and quite possibly cause loss of a job shortly after the trainee is placed. But the same comment could be made about nearly every occupational field.

Upcoming change and its effects are just as relevant to other forms of training, for example, at the college and university level. A good part of our focus should be on the *quality* of training being given, so that the person becomes as flexible and responsive to change as possible. It may very well be that many will have to be retrained more than once and that we are really moving, in an evolutionary way, to a continuum of training efforts at all levels during our working lives.

8. When all is said and done, any training effort has to be based on the people involved—their skills, aptitudes, interests, previous work experience, and educational attainment. The interplay of this dimension with the availability of jobs represents the major context in which our programs have to be carried out. Thus we have approved programs for waiters, because a demonstrated job need was shown, the skill content and a corresponding curriculum were demonstrated, and unemployed men were found whose aptitudes, interests, and backgrounds made for a favorable prognosis. Similarly, we are continuing to approve training programs in the farm sector where we have successfully trained underemployed migrant workers as year-round farm machinery operators.

9. Now we come to the characteristics of the trainees themselves. With the caveat, again, that data for those actually enrolled in courses are based on relatively small numbers, here are some of the highlights:

The first 10,000 actual enrollees under MDTA were distributed by age as follows:

Total	100.0%
Under 19 years	4.4
19–21	20.0
22–34	43.1
35–44	22.1
45 and over	10.5

Under provisions of the act, youths under 19 may take training but may not receive allowances during their training period. Youths 19 through 21 (unless otherwise eligible by virtue of the fact that they are family heads, have had the required amount of labor force experience, and so on) may receive limited training allowances up to a maximum of $20 a week. As the brief summary table shows, about one-fourth of the first 10,000 trainees were youths under 22; this is just about the same proportion as found among all unemployed.

About two-thirds were in the age range 22 to 44, although this category accounts for only 40 per cent of the unemployed. Correspondingly, those 45 years of age and over made up about 10 per cent of enrolled trainees but account for about 30 per cent of all unemployed. So far, at least, we are falling short on providing a proportionate share of training for the older workers. A much greater effort will be needed in terms of job development, design of courses, and acceptance of older workers by employers.

10. Among our first enrolled 10,000 trainees, we find the following educational attainment:

Total	100.0%
Less than 8 years of school	2.8
8 years	6.9
9–11 years	27.8
12 years	52.5
Over 12 years	10.0

Thus about six out of every ten enrolled trainees have had a high school education or better; four out of ten do not have a high school diploma and, of those, one in ten never got beyond grade school. The proportion of those with a high school education or better is, perhaps, not surprising in view of the occupational distribution we have already noted. Moreover, they are more likely to survive the guidance, counseling, and testing processes before selection and referral for training.

11. Given the requirements of the act and the realities of the labor force, it was predictable that a disproportionately small number of persons with low educational attainment would be enrolled. This can be particularly true where only a relatively small percentage of the total unemployed can be trained under

current and immediately foreseeable funding. It would, in fact, be relatively easy to skim the cream of the unemployed and enroll those with the best prognosis for successful placement. To date, the enrollment figures indicate that this has been done. It has led us to design and support special programs, many of them frankly experimental, which aim specifically at disadvantaged groups.

Thus there was a course in Hammonton, New Jersey, which included training in the operation, maintenance, and repair of tractors and tractor implements, together with job-oriented arithmetic and English language instruction. The 25 trainees, most of whom were Spanish-speaking migratory workers, followed another group, all members of which were succesfully placed at substantially higher wages and annual earnings than they had formerly enjoyed.

We have entered into agreements with private agencies in such areas as New Haven, New York City, and Portsmouth, Virginia, for the guidance, counseling, testing, and training of particularly disadvantaged groups, with very low educational attainment, many on relief rolls. These programs are supported in part by our research funds and will serve as demonstration projects on the feasibility of moving into meaningful training and retraining programs for these sectors of our population.

There have been enough of these operations to permit expressing the opinion that, while "functional illiteracy" and similar ailments of some unemployed are very difficult barriers, they are not insurmountable; and that it is absolutely necessary to overcome them in a free and democratic society. We must show that it can be done. We may fail in some cases, but we are taking seriously the urgings for "new approaches, new methods, bold efforts."

12. Data are available to show unemployment experience of the first 6,000 trainees.

Total	100.0%
Unemployed less than	
5 weeks	26.2
5–14 weeks	24.3
15–26 weeks	15.9
27–52 weeks	12.6
More than 52 weeks	21.0

It is encouraging that one of every five trainees had been out of work for more than a year but did get selected for retraining. In fact, about 50 per cent of this first group met the official definition of long-term unemployment (15 weeks or more)—nearly double the corresponding proportion among the total unemployed.

13. The placement rate among those who have completed training is 71 per cent. Our warning about small numbers is particularly apt here, in view of the fact that data are available for only about 2,000 completions. These programs began not much more than six months ago and the average duration of training programs is close to six months; the maximum allowable with support by training allowances is 52 weeks. Whether the placement rate will continue to be this high remains to be seen. For those who want some standard against which to measure this rate of placement, it may be noted that ongoing vocational courses which deal predominantly with the young have a placement rate of about 80 per cent. Sweden, with a very low unemployment level, mobility allowances, and a much longer period of retraining experience, has a placement rate of 75 per cent in its programs.

14. Like all other education and training programs, those operated under MDTA also have dropouts. Here, too, the data are minimal, but they show a dropout rate of less than 15 per cent, a low rate in comparison with any other known programs in the regular high school, post-high school, or adult training systems. If this low rate continues, it will testify to the strength of motivation on the part of these unemployed family heads.

Dropouts occur for a wide and familiar variety of reasons ranging from job offers, illness, persistent absence, marriage and pregnancy to death.

15. Of particular concern is the inadequacy of training allowances in many cases. Under the law, an eligible person may receive an amount equivalent to the average unemployment insurance payment prevailing in his state. If his own record in covered employment warrants a higher payment, he does, of course, receive that. The average for the United States is $35 a week; the range is from $22 to $43 for the 50 states.

The problem comes to the fore particularly when a person has to sign up for a substantial period of time during which he can receive only his training allowance. Any earnings from work done outside training time are deducted from his allowance. In six states this means that he will receive less than $100 a month; in practically all states, less than $150 a month. Since the majority of trainees are family heads, a commitment to a long period of training with this kind of income can be an important constraint. We already have a significant number of trainees who have dropped out because they could not support their families on the allowances. Some were trying to hold a job while training, found the conflict in hours impossible, and dropped out in favor of the job they held. In other cases family members delayed entry into college to take a job while the family head was taking training.

16. As operations have progressed, we have come face to face with some of the realities of the training situation in this country, particularly in the shortage of qualified vocational educational facilities and teachers. Under MDTA we may support the training effort through funds for needed additional equipment, rent, light, and salaries of instructors. In several states, however, delay and even cancellation of approved programs has been occasioned by lack of facilities with space and personnel to carry out the required training.

17. As indicated at the beginning, programs under MDTA are being consummated by ongoing institutional arrangements, through the operations of state and local educational and employment security agencies. Thus we have a tremendous head start because their experience, facilities, and contacts can be used. One cannot see how these varied programs could have gotten under way without the existence of a vocational education system in the locality, with the know-how, the facilities, and, perhaps most important, the ability to get the necessary teachers. Much the same is true for the local employment service office with its knowledge of the labor market, its counseling and testing facilities, its knowledge of the unemployed.

One of the best developments that may come out of the first years under MDTA is a closer link, at the local level, between those in charge of designing and providing education and those in charge of designing and providing effective labor market programs. The potential benefits to both the educational and employment security systems are incalculable.

These, then, are some of the points which emerge at the early stages of operations under MDTA. Much more will be learned in the months ahead as more complete data on many more cases become available. And we shall be undertaking many other items of evaluation as the programs develop: why some drop out before completion; why some are not selected for training to begin with; whether placement occurs in jobs which are related to the training received; how well the person does on the job. Also to be examined is the role of mobility in relation to these training programs. Unlike the Trade Expansion Act, MDTA does not provide for aiding in the movement of workers; and the importance of this factor will be carefully reviewed in the near future.

Discussion

E. WIGHT BAKKE

The period since the training programs have been in effect is so short that any criticism of their results or even of their structure or administration would be untimely. They have hardly had time to "take their shakedown cruises" yet.

We welcome the efforts being made thus far on the retraining program by the responsible people in the Department of Labor and the Department of Health, Education, and Welfare in Washington and in the states and local communities. They should be given the chance to show what they can do before we start criticizing or suggesting how they could do it better.

There is one question, however, about this relatively new emphasis on training and retraining as a part of the whole roster of *public* manpower services. Is it possible that this program can serve broader objectives than its unquestioned service to individual unemployed workers? Can the effort be made an integral part, a genuinely supporting part, of a well-coordinated, overall, positive, labor market policy and program, aiming to make maximum use of our manpower potential for the nation's economic health and growth?

The statement of purpose in the MDTA expresses exactly the intention. That statement is a broadly gauged declaration that manpower development is to become a key aspect of the total public effort to marshal every economic resource we have to promote strength and growth in the economy. The hopes and expectations that are being raised by the publicity accompanying the early stages of the program are focused on the possible impact of the program in helping to eliminate this black mark of 5 to 6 per cent unemployment on our economic record. Those who are responsible for planning and administering the program have an enthusiasm and morale that is based on the belief that they are making such a contribution. This, therefore, is no criticism of them. It grows out of a desire to think *with* them on how these high hopes can be realized.

There is one way that this retraining program helps to reduce unemployment for particular individuals if not the aggregate amount. It will obviously help individuals who are unemployed to find jobs they would not have had, making the program worth all its costs. Criticisms that it does not really hold out hope for *all* the unemployed, the hard core, for instance, or that it is a drop in the bucket in the light of the volume of unemployment in certain depressed areas, or that only 16,000 out of 127,000 who were tested were found capable of taking the training offered, are from this point of view beside the point. If it turns out that the 16,000 trained obtain jobs they would not have had otherwise, there will have been real achievement in terms of the chance of these 16,000 to contribute by their work to their own, their families', and the nation's economic well-being.

But, if the program is to be an integral and useful part of an active manpower program making a real and major contribution to the full employment commitment, it would seem that the objectives, and hence the direction and concept, of the program will have to go beyond this unquestionably useful and worthy achievement of helping a necessarily limited number of unemployed to better work and a better life.

Let us think about this matter a bit. What guide lines might be suggested *then* for emphases that could enlarge the horizons of the training program from one of relief to individual unemployed to encompass a contribution to a positive labor market and manpower program, which in turn contributes to an overall attempt to move nearer to full employment, economic strength, and growth for the nation?

The success of the effort to approximate full employment rides on the creation of *new* jobs. It is not enough to move presently unemployed people after retraining into jobs, for example, clerical or even semiskilled industrial jobs, which ordinarily might have been taken up by new youthful entrants into the labor market. Now economists generally are convinced that the big push in creating *new* jobs will come from demand expanding measures related to monetary and fiscal and investment policy. But is there anything a training and retraining program can do in this area?

One thing that slows down economic expansion is actual shortages of people ready to perform in certain skilled bottleneck occupations. If those bottlenecks could be broken, thus reducing the inhibitions facing entrepreneurial management to expand or initiate enterprise requiring such skilled performance, not only could employment increase in these skilled occupations, but also the establishment or expansion of the total enterprise of which they are a part would be likely to create more openings for less skilled people who also have to be employed in such productive enterprise.

Now it does not seem likely that a program of retraining for the unemployed to get them ready, even in 52 weeks, for work which promises to be available in the local labor market will reduce those shortages of highly skilled people. Aside from those who are able to afford formal training in, say, engineering for several years, the best candidates for training for those jobs are not the unemployed, but people already employed at jobs providing a foundation in know-how and experience upon which training for upgrading to those jobs can be based. But how would training employed people help the unemployed? What might be envisaged here is a chain-reaction upgrading which would create openings down the skill levels which the unemployed could be more likely to fill with the kind of minimal retraining which is related to their skill potential and the limited public resources available for such retraining.

What is being suggested here is that a retraining program which is a part of a positive manpower program would be concerned not merely with training for existing unfilled local job openings for which existing locally unemployed workers had the skill potential to be trained. It would also be concerned with amplifying retraining for presently employed people so they could be upgraded to fill job shortages, which then would create job openings down the line until the skill level was reached which is realistically consistent with that which the unemployed after retraining could bring to the openings thus created.

Such a program entails an emphasis on *in-plant* training. No one would suggest, of course, that the government should pay for the training that General Motors gives to 7,200 workers a year so that they can be upgraded to skilled jobs for which General Motors would have an insufficient supply were it not for that program. Nor is it suggested that the government absorb IBM's cost for its program of training tens of thousands a year to service and educate in the use of their equipment and for other functions making possible the expansion of the production of their product. Other large corporations with the ability to implement their foresight and ambitions for expansion in this way are doing the same. Is it not possible, however, that the economic patriotism of many of these firms could be stimulated, with the training facilities, equipment, and faculty they have available, to expand their training effort, with government subsidies, for the purpose of providing firms *other than their own* with persons capable of reducing *their* bottlenecks in highly skilled workers?

Another factor which inhibits investment in new enterprise, and hence in newly created jobs, particularly for ambitious *but small-scale* risk takers, is the cost of training workers in communities where workers but not the required skills are readily available. Could a system of cooperation from government through a partial support of their training program encourage these risk takers to take the plunge and hence get under way productive enterprise that promises opening up new jobs not only in the present but in the future also as these enterprises grow? Training costs are not, of course, as dominant a consideration as a number of other costs in influencing investment decision making, but any reduction in those costs is a positive influence in the right direction.

Incidentally, in supplying such training assistance to new and expanding industry, the present MDTA is overly restrictive by limiting the proportion of training allowances which can be paid to youths between 19 and 22 to 5 per cent of the estimated annual total. Experience alone will tell, but, for many jobs, employer preferences for the younger trainees will probably become evident.

Even though the dominant public effort toward creating new job openings will probably continue to be related to fiscal, monetary, and investment programs, there is, in making entrepreneurship more likely in expanding and new industrial enterprise, a role for public training and retraining programs.

As a part of a positive manpower program, training effort would be concerned with long- as well as short-range labor force development. One thing which would characterize a training effort guided by the objective to contribute positively to continued economic strength and growth would be the provision of a general

grounding in the basic sciences on which new industrial processes are going to rest. Existing vocational training of both the
private apprentice and in-plant and institutional trade school types
tend to prepare the trainees for immediate performance in particular narrow occupational areas. If there is anything which is
clear to the students of our manpower problems and the administrators of our public manpower programs, it is that the expect-
ancy anyone can have of continuing for a whole working life
without facing major changes in the skill content in, or the actual
disappearance of, the occupation for which one has been trained
is diminishing to the vanishing point. Vocational and apprenticeship training in the past could count on this probability to continuity in job requirement to validate their emphasis on fairly
specialized retraining. The hallmark of adequate vocational and
apprenticeship training in the future promises to be training for
adaptation to change, which implies more emphasis on basic
scientific principles than in the past.

It is not suggested that the public training efforts provide a
wholesale development of courses in basic science, but that they
stimulate in every way possible—in the development of public
vocational, and private apprenticeship and in-plant training—the
broadening of the content base of courses with this adaptability
of skill in mind.

There are already signs that one of the happy consequences of
the initiation of federal training and retraining programs is that
they bring knowledge of the labor market and labor force to the
attention of the institutional and in-plant vocational training
people. This can be accomplished informally through the requirements established for federally supported courses and through
demonstration projects. For example, in England the Ministry of
Labor has already demonstrated that a one-year basic general
pre-apprenticeship program can reduce actual on-the-job apprenticeship training from 4–6 to 2–4 years. The suggestion made here
is that the effort of public manpower people to update the con-
ception of the scope and imperatives of vocational and apprenticeship training among those who are always going to be the
numerically most dominant trainees be considered not merely a
fortunate by-product but a major concern and emphasis of the
public training and retraining effort.

Finally, it may be suggested that a training program that can lay claim to being a major significant aspect of the entire public effort to move toward full employment, economic health, and growth will increasingly be oriented to the national rather than merely to local labor market needs and possibilities. The proclamation of intent to do so is implicit in the MDTA and explicit in the declarations of purpose made by those in charge of administering the act. As yet, there is not much indication of the way that intent is going to be brought out into life. The act itself in its wise provision, during this experimental stage, that training courses in particular communities shall be geared to probable job openings (usually job openings in the same communities) tends to focus concern primarily on the local labor market. The hesitancy to pay traveling and removal allowances results in the same limitation. To the extent that, after the second year, costs will be shared by the states, local pressures for spending local funds only when local benefits are obvious will become stronger.

These suggestions as to how policy, plans, and performance might move in the direction of making the retraining effort not simply a service to individual unemployed but an integral part of an overall labor market program have been merely illustrative. Let us merely mention five of the implications of such a development:

1. Although such an emphasis can be administered through a federal-state system, the funds will have to come predominantly if not entirely from federal sources.

2. The *major* breakthrough is likely to come, not from the present type of institutional training, but from marshaling the self-interest, the facilities, the instructors, and the probable availability of jobs that are present in the case of amplified in-plant training.

3. An enlarged emphasis on the basic, and not narrow, training of youth would be required with an eye not only on preparation for specific occupational tasks but also on the need for adaptation to future shifts in the skill content and the actual disappearance of present-day occupations.

4. Since government efforts will always be marginal to the great volume of private effort in this business of training and retraining for work, heavy support can well be given to demonstra-

tion projects indicating new paths for private efforts to follow.

5. Manpower vocational development as a major part of public economic policy and program is still in its infancy, and there is a real challenge here to the foresight and initiative of public servants who have a chance to participate in bringing it to maturity.

NATHANIEL GOLDFINGER

If we are to make up for lost time and to achieve rapid progress in policy and program formulation, we need a rigorous re-examination of our problems, our analyses and efforts. Search for scapegoats will not prove helpful, for all of us have blinded ourselves to the realities as they have unfolded since the end of the Korean War. One need only mention society's crime against the coal miners and textile workers in 1953–1957, with hardly a murmur of protest except from those directly affected, while most of academia, like most of the rest of us, concentrated attention on a general demand—inflation that was long since gone.

Employment and labor market policy should be at the center of economic thinking, for manpower is our most precious resource, and the satisfaction of human beings is, or should be, a basic goal of national policy. In attempting to re-focus our thinking on employment and labor market policy, there is need for an integrated framework of analyses, policies, programs, goals, and priorities— in other words, an integrated full employment policy. Such a framework and policy we do not yet have.

The goal is full employment and one can agree with Wolfbein's textual definition. While this vague goal may be satisfactory at the moment, it is not an adequate long-term objective for national policy. But, to spell out the definition in a meaningful way for policy making, we need the kinds of labor market studies we do not have: studies that can provide us with an approximate measurement, in terms of the special conditions of the American labor market, of a minimum level of unemployment below which it would be hard to get even with active demand and labor market policies. Such a minimum level is probably in the neighborhood of an unemployment rate of 2 to 2½ per cent. It is a reflection on the sad disarray in American economic thinking of recent years that the goal of full employment has so often been defined in terms of the price level, rather than as a function of the labor market.

But there are other issues of greater importance at this time. In 1963, with an unemployment rate of 5½ to 6 per cent, the priority emphasis should be on a sustained effort to reduce unemployment as rapidly as possible.

As Professor Haber and Dr. Wolfbein have said, the causes of the high and rising levels of unemployment of the past decade are varied. But this crucial issue deserves more serious examination, in depth, than it has received to date. Adequate diagnosis is an essential prerequisite for an adequate remedy.

The major underlying problem is a continuing deficiency of aggregate demand in relation to the economy's increasing ability to produce. This has been true ever since 1953, with the possible exception of a few months at the end of 1955 and early in 1956. But related to this deficiency in aggregate demand are the depressing effects of shifts in the demand-mix—connected with such factors as changes in demography and consumer preference, radical shifts in defense technology, the increased importance of personal and business services, regressive trends in income distribution, and a slowdown of major innovations in the civilian economy.

Aggregate fiscal and monetary policies are an essential ingredient. But monolithic reliance on the aggregate approach alone cannot be the sole key to the solution of our problem—not only because of changes in the demand-mix, but also because of growing structural problems in the labor market. Professor Haber and Dr. Wolfbein have indicated generally what these problems are: rapid technological change in several key parts of the economy, the obsolescence of old skills and declining requirements for unskilled and semiskilled workers, the decline and/or relocation of companies and industries.

If there is any validity to this cursory diagnosis, our actual policies and programs in the past decade have been strange indeed. Instead of top-priority emphasis on the expansion of aggregate demand and the development of programs to offset the depressing effects of shifts in the demand-mix, we have consistently, since 1953, encouraged and stimulated savings and subsidized investment in new plants and equipment, thereby aggravating the problem of under-utilization and contributing to the regressive shift in the distribution of income and wealth.

Since January 1961, spokesmen for the Administration have usually posed the under-utilization problem as one that is due overwhelmingly, or even solely, to demand deficiency. But the actual programs and policies of the past two years have been essentially aimed at structural problems—the Area Redevelopment Act, the Manpower Development and Training Act, the adjustment procedures of the Trade Expansion Act.

The cart has been put before the horse, and political realities create pressures for these much-belated programs to provide success stories. Instead of an integrated attack on the unemployment problem, we now have a developing proliferation of agencies and programs, sometimes overlapping and sometimes competing, in an attempt to solve structural problems in an environment of high unemployment.

There are a host of other problems that confront us in employment and labor market policies, in addition to these basic inconsistencies. Because we have been so late in getting started on an active labor market policy, we lack experience, precedent, and trained personnel. In addition, we are engaged in tokenism rather than in massive efforts to reduce unemployment—not only in relation to demand, but also in relation to structural problems.

Even the numbers that are supposed to impress us with the successes of ARA and MDTA are pitifully small in relation to the serious problem. Moreover, when we look at the figures, such as the data presented by Dr. Wolfbein, it does not seem as if much emphasis has been placed on increasing the skill level of the labor force and on meeting the skill needs of an economy in the throes of radical technological change. And the base of our training program—the vocational education system, on which training and retraining must rest—is as poor as or poorer than Professor Haber has described.

In a rational labor market policy, an effective nation-wide employment service would be at the center. But, even with the improvements in the employment service of the past two years, we have never had, except during the war, a national employment service with a labor market orientation. Such a service has been needed throughout the postwar period. It is even more necessary at present. A public relations approach alone cannot achieve the national employment service we need. At a minimum, clear federal standards and federal policy direction of the employment service are required, and probably companies operating on federal contracts should be required to place their job openings with the employment service.

The federal-state-local relationships present difficulties in training and retraining, in vocational education, and in area redevelopment, as well as in the employment service. These are practical realities which we must confront squarely. But, unless we develop some clear set of federal standards and basic federal nation-wide policy guide lines—in manpower training, vocational and technical education, in area redevelopment, and in the all-important employment service—we shall continue merely to play around the periphery of structural unemployment problems, with a scattered proliferation of policies and programs, even if the economy should achieve a higher rate of economic growth.

There have been some improvements in the employment service in the past two years. There are several good local vocational education systems. There are some examples of genuine achievements by ARA, and there are also a number of very good MDTA retraining programs. But, thus far, they tend to be isolated cases rather than the general rule, and we are still far away, in actual practice, from an integrated employment and labor market policy in this nation.

We have permitted a trend toward a polarization of the population—perhaps as much as half of the labor force, essentially production and maintenance types of workers, who are subject to frequent unemployment and part-time work, who have suffered severe income losses, who are generally subjected to very slow improvements in real incomes, and who are simultaneously lectured about wage restraints, costs, prices, and the balance-of-payments problems. At the other end is a group of about 20 per cent of the labor force consisting of managerial, professional, and higher paid technical personnel—with rising employment opportunities, rapidly increasing incomes and capital gains, who are not faced with guide lines for their income improvements or with appeals for restraint. This condition, attributable in large part to the slow rate of economic growth and high unemployment, is a potential threat to our society.

First, we need expansionary fiscal and monetary policies to boost substantially the demand for goods, services, and manpower.

Secondly, we need the development of programs to offset the depressing effects of recent shifts in the demand-mix—probably in the area of substantial increases in job-creating and materials-utilizing public investment programs, such as urban redevelopment and mass transportation. Related to such efforts, we also need specific job-creating programs for youth and for the long-term unemployed, those unskilled and semiskilled workers who have been displaced by radical technological change and find retraining impossible or difficult.

Thirdly, we need a meaningful and active labor market policy, including relocation allowances for workers. Such an active labor market policy should be an integrated part of an overall full employment policy.

But, in all of this, tokenism will not do. Unemployment is a serious economic and social problem. Massive, genuine efforts are needed to create jobs, to revive depressed areas to the extent that it is possible, to encourage labor mobility, and to upgrade the skills of the labor force to meet the skill requirements of the radical technological changes of this decade. And underlying such massive efforts must be a national, integrated employment and labor market policy—a meaningful full employment policy that is actually enforced.

GERALD G. SOMERS

There can be little disagreement with the major conclusions reached by Professor Haber and Dr. Wolfbein in their excellent evaluations of retraining and labor market policies.* The Department of Labor officials responsible for evaluation of the MDTA

* Portions of this discussion are derived from research conducted under a grant from the Ford Foundation to evaluate programs for retraining and relocating unemployed workers.

reach many of the same conclusions in their first annual report on the act; and these points are reiterated in the *Manpower Report of the President,* issued a few weeks ago.* Several recent newspaper accounts and magazine articles have drawn a roughly similar picture.

On the whole, the conclusions reached by Professor Haber and other critics are disheartening. They are disheartening not because retraining lacks potential for long-run good but because the programs to date appear to be having such limited short-run impact on the hard core of unemployment. The disillusionment is greater because the initial expectations were so high. In the various Congressional hearings on unemployment policies, retraining proposals met with an almost "unanimous chorus of praise." After all, training is education, and who can be opposed to education? Training is the vehicle for occupational mobility, and in a dynamic economy of structural change who can be opposed to mobility?

But the expectations and current experience must both be seen in perspective. Retraining has three major functions: (1) short-run increase in employment; (2) long-run economic growth; (3) improvement in the welfare and general well-being of the trainees and society. Regardless of any short-run deficiencies, there can be little doubt that retraining the unemployed is a worthwhile enterprise from the standpoints of the long-run economic growth of the American economy and the general well-being of its citizens. In fact, some authorities are now saying that the investment in human resources, through education and training, has accounted for a greater part of our economic growth than the investment in capital equipment. Even if immediate employment does not result, the acquisition of new skills and knowledge by the unemployed is likely to make some future contribution to their own advancement and that of the economy.

Retraining allowances will usually take the place of unemploy-

* *Report of the Secretary of Labor on Research and Training Activities Under the Manpower Development and Training Act,* U. S. Department of Labor, February 1963, especially pp. 63–65; *Manpower Report of the President and a Report on Manpower Requirements, The Sources, Utilization and Training,* U. S. Department of Labor, March 1963, especially pp. 115–116.

ment compensation or relief payments for unemployed workers. Given these small additions to the costs for society, in what better way can the unemployed spend their moments of enforced idleness than in the acquisition of new skills? Our research provides ample evidence that retraining can give a new sense of pride, confidence, and social status to unemployed workers; and these represent substantial social gains regardless of immediate labor market consequences.

Therefore a greatly expanded program for retraining of the unemployed should be favored even if it could be demonstrated that no immediate jobs were created thereby. Professor Haber and Dr. Wolfbein would probably share this view. But most of those who have supported recent retraining measures have been more concerned with the current problems of unemployment than with long-run growth and well-being. And herein lies the disillusionment. The short-run concern can be seen in the MDTA provisions which restrict retraining to those who have "a reasonable expectation of employment"; in the incorporation of retraining provisions in the ARA attack on depressed areas; in the inclusion of retraining to meet the dislocations which may result from the Trade Expansion Act; in the retraining provisions espoused in the Youth Conservation Bill; and in the many state and local efforts to reduce relief rolls through retraining.

And, yet, retraining has achieved only minor reductions in unemployment to date. Professor Haber and other critics have noted deficiencies in the current programs; and our own research, although still in process, supports many of these findings. Some deficiencies are minor. They are recognized by the training authorities and can be corrected with the passage of time. Our responses from trainees, employers, unions, and government officials indicate that some of the current ARA and MDTA courses are too short for the occupational objectives they seek to achieve; equipment is often inadequate in quantity and quality, and frequently it is available to unemployed trainees for only a few hours in the evening; instructors may be out of touch with the latest techniques; training allowances are often inadequate; retrained workers are not provided the tools which they are expected to bring to the job; local advisory committees have not always functioned effectively; the complicated relations between the Office of Manpower, Automation, and Training, the Bureau of Employment Security, and Health, Education, and Welfare—both in Washington and at the local level—have sometimes served to delay the inception of programs and impair their effective functioning.

These are growing pains, however, and they can be expected to diminish as greater experience is gained. The relatively meager accomplishments of the retraining programs to date are understandable because they have just begun, but the real concern for their future success stems from more fundamental causes. Although these have been touched on by Professor Haber and Dr. Wolfbein, a few points raised by them deserve greater emphasis.

Immediate employment effects of retraining

To what extent have the present government retraining programs really created more jobs for the unemployed and to what extent are they likely to do so in the future? This is obviously a very basic question, and it can be fully answered only with much more research and a longer period of analysis. Some pertinent considerations are merely suggested here.

First, government-subsidized retraining of unemployed workers will create immediate employment only if vacancies exist which would not be filled in the absence of the retraining programs. It is frequently pointed out that there are still shortage occupations in spite of the large volume of unemployment. The shortages are said to occur at four levels: first, the professional level—scientists, engineers, teachers; second, the lower technical level, such as laboratory assistants, data processors, keypunchers, and draftsmen; third, the skilled manual trades, such as electricians, automobile mechanics, and building craftsmen; and fourth, low-level service trades, such as waitresses and nurses aides. The professional categories are clearly beyond the scope of the present retraining programs because of the time required for the completion of training and the inadequate educational preparation of most of the unemployed.

If shortages exist at the two intermediate levels, and if the vacancies can be filled by training workers in courses ranging from 16 to 52 weeks, in the ARA and MDTA programs, why are the shortages not filled by the training programs of private employers? On-the-job training, apprentice training, and other varieties of these private programs have traditionally been used to fill shortages, and they continue to be the most widespread form of occupational training in the United States. A Department of Labor survey conducted among more than 710,000 establishments in the spring of 1962 found that 2½ million workers were actually being trained in these establishments at that time.* Three-fourths of all establishments with 500 or more employees had training programs. These data are to be compared with the few thousand that have been trained under the ARA and MDTA to date, and even with the 400,000 to be trained under the MDTA's total three-year program.

If employers are not training workers to fill the shortages at the intermediate occupational levels, it must be because they feel that the shortages are not sufficiently great or persistent or the qualifications of potential trainees are not sufficiently promising to warrant the training investment. In some cases the investment would involve the establishment of training facilities. Since employers fail to undertake an upgrading program to fill shortages by drawing from among their own employees, they are even less likely to hire and retrain unemployed workers for the intermediate job vacancies.

Under these circumstances a government program of retraining will induce employers to hire formerly unemployed workers only if the government program represents a sufficient subsidy. The subsidy must be large enough to induce the employer to fill a vacancy which he would not fill if left to his own devices. Only then can we say that the government retraining program has created employment.

The low-level service occupations represent a different kind of shortage. Here the shortage is related to low wages, undesirable working conditions, and high turnover. The retraining subsidy in this case is more crucial for the worker than for the employer. Hospitals are willing to hire nurses' aides and orderlies with minimal skills and training. But how to induce workers to acquire even this minimal skill for a job which they do not consider very desirable in the first place? Training allowances provide an incentive to undertake such training courses, and the trainees are

* *Manpower Report of the President,* p. 197.

thereby placed under some obligation to accept the job for which they have been trained. Unfortunately, our follow-up surveys indicate that, having benefited from the training allowance during the course, many of the trainees stay on the hospital job for only a short time after completion of their training. The shortages then continue in spite of the training program. As Dr. Wolfbein has noted, the major contribution that the government programs can make here is the possible inducement of higher wages and better conditions commensurate with the higher productivity of the trainees.

A second basic problem, related to the question of immediate job creation, is the failure of the current programs to get at the older worker, the under-educated, and the minorities—the truly hard core of the unemployed. Perhaps the most striking evidence of this failure is seen in the age comparison between MDTA trainees and the long-term unemployed as a whole. Only 8.9 per cent of the male trainees enrolled in 1962 were over 45 years of age, whereas 31.9 per cent of all males unemployed six months or longer in 1962 were over 45.* A similar contrast is found in the age composition of ARA trainees and the age composition of all unemployed in the depressed areas to which ARA is directed.

It is generally conceded that greater experimentation must take place in formulating retraining programs for older workers and the ill-educated. These characteristics are often found in the same persons. The many functional illiterates found among the unemployed cannot hope to pass the screening interview or understand the aptitude test for retraining, let alone handle the content of the training course itself in any but the low-level service occupations. Efforts to educate and retrain these people are clearly desirable from the standpoints of long-run economic growth and general well-being.

But, will the extension of retraining to the hard core make any substantial contribution to immediate job creation in the present economy? It must be noted that only 60 per cent of the ARA trainees and 70 per cent of the MDTA trainees are now being placed on jobs, even under the current selective recruiting standards. It is likely that the placement ratio would drop still further if selection criteria were changed to include more older, ill-edu-

* *Ibid.,* p. 47, and *Report of the Secretary of Labor on MDTA,* p. 55.

cated, and minority groups. In the terminology used above, the subsidy inducement to employers would have to be raised still further to overcome their traditional attitudes to the hiring of workers in these categories.

This leads to a third fundamental problem of job placement in the retraining field—the anomalous role of the Employment Service. Can the Service be expected to reduce its standards for the selection of trainees as long as its success rating in Congress and elsewhere depends on its job placement ratio? Certainly, if the hard core of the unemployed are to be included in the retraining programs, the Employment Service's contribution to the programs must be judged in terms other than the success of immediate job placement.

On the other hand, given the Service's present selective standards for trainee recruits, and its efforts to make a good showing in job placement, can we be sure that a job obtained after retraining results from the skills acquired in the training course? Professor Haber finds justification for the retraining programs in the job placement of unemployed workers after completion of their course. It can certainly be held that even if only 60 to 70 per cent of the trainees are placed, the programs must be considered a worthwhile venture on the score of job creation. The big unanswered question is whether these workers—the cream of the unemployed—would have obtained a job just as readily if they had been bypassed in training but were given the same treatment as the trainees in careful testing, selection, and placement efforts by the Employment Service.

Surveys among employers indicate that the careful screening and selection of trainees by the Employment Service is a major influence on the employer's willingness to hire them. Often the actual skills acquired in the course play a secondary role. Employers are also influenced by the special placement efforts made on behalf of the trainees by the Employment Service. Trying to establish a good record under the new program, many of the local offices have given special emphasis to the placement of trainees. A case in point is the ARA program in Huntington, West Virginia— the first in the nation. After national criticism for an initially poor placement record, the local employment office was urged to make greater efforts to find jobs for the trainees, and it succeeded in raising the placement ratio above the national average for other ARA programs.

Some policy recommendations

Of the many policy recommendations which might be offered for the future course of MDTA retraining, three questions stemming from the analysis above deserve greater emphasis than they have been given: the role to be played by on-the-job training; the most effective relationship between retraining and relocation; and the relationship of retraining and accelerated economic growth.

1. The immediate employment effects resulting from government-subsidized retraining could be enhanced by subsidized on-the-job training. The on-the-job training provisions of the MDTA are just now in the process of being implemented for the first time since passage of the act over a year ago. However, a number of the ARA retraining programs have been so closely geared to the needs of a single employer that they provide a useful experience by which to judge the advantages, as well as some of the pitfalls, of on-the-job training for the unemployed.

By definition, the immediate job placement record of retraining will be greater if the unemployed are hired even before they are trained. The trainee benefits in morale by being assured of employment, and the employer is provided with employees trained to the specifications of his particular job. The subsidy to the employer embodied in government-financed retraining can be a more direct and more attractive inducement to his expansion of employment opportunities when he gains greater control of the retraining procedures and content. Our surveys indicate that many employers, especially in such service occupations as auto repair and nurses' aides, would prefer this type of arrangement. In view of the slow start of the MDTA and the continuing shortage of vocational school facilities and instructors, it is not likely that the goal of 400,000 trainees can be achieved in three years without widespread use of on-the-job training.

But caution must be observed to ensure that much of the training is extended to unemployed workers and not only to the upgrading of existing employees. Our analysis indicates that many employers might prefer to use the government-subsidized retraining provisions in ways which offer little benefit for the unemployed. The recently issued manual of procedure for on-the-job training under MDTA does not appear to include sufficient safeguards on this point. Care must also be taken to see that employees are assured some continuity of employment after their government-subsidized on-the-job training. Workers trained for a specific job in a specific plant will be placed in a vulnerable position if they are again set adrift among the unemployed. There have been some unfortunate experiences along this line under ARA programs geared to a specific employer. Here, too, the manual of procedure for MDTA on-the-job training does not appear to provide adequate safeguards.

2. Relocation of retrained workers will frequently be necessary if the retraining investment is to bear fruit in job placement. This is especially true of retraining in depressed areas. It is not always recognized that the acquisition of new skills through a retraining program is in itself a powerful inducement to move out of an area of limited employment opportunities. In a study of McDowell County, West Virginia—a depressed coal mining area—it was found that almost one-third of the trainees under a state program for the unemployed had moved out of the county by the time of the survey. Over 100 of the West Virginia outmigrants were tracked down through mail questionnaires and personal interviews. In a preliminary tabulation, over 40 per cent indicated that their decision to move had been influenced by their training. However, only half of these were employed, as compared with 60 per cent of the total outmigrant group and roughly the same percentage who found employment under all ARA retraining programs.

One lesson to be learned here is that the major role of relocation allowances should be not to induce *more* outmigration but rather a *more rational* outmigration. By making the allowance contingent upon a move to known job opportunities, much fruitless geographic movement could be avoided. A second lesson is directly related to the planning of training programs in depressed areas. Less than 3 per cent of the outmigrants were over 50 years of age. Training courses for unskilled older workers should be mainly in low service occupations, geared to local opportunities. Younger workers in depressed areas should be given training in welding or some of the expanding intermediate occupations which presuppose their migration to areas in which industrial growth is taking place.

3. Finally, retraining can do little to provide employment opportunities unless it is accompanied by vigorous policies designed to accelerate the rate of overall economic growth. It is a point that "structuralists" all recognize and the "aggregate demand school" constantly repeats. But little attention is given in research or policy implementation to the changing requirements of the retraining programs as economic growth accelerates and we approach full employment. The closer we come to full employment, under expansionary monetary-fiscal policy, the greater will be the number of job vacancies and the need for retraining. But it can be expected that employers will then be willing to conduct more of this retraining themselves and the subsidy provided by the government programs may be less essential for increasing overall employment levels.

As we approach full employment, the role of government-subsidized retraining can and should change—and the change should be reflected in the types of courses approved. The emphasis should shift from the immediate creation of employment through retraining to the most efficient utilization and allocation of manpower resources in continuing long-run economic growth. This is the major contribution to be made by government subsidies in the labor market.

THE PROBLEM OF
EXPANDING ECONOMIC ACTIVITY

PART II

THE PROBLEM OF
EXPANDING ECONOMIC ACTIVITY

CHAPTER 4

The Administration's Fiscal Policy

BY WALTER W. HELLER

The case for vigorous measures to expand aggregate demand seems self-evident in an economy with 5½ to 6 per cent unemployment, with output well below both capacity and preferred operating rates, and with GNP at $572 billion when it could readily be $600 to $610 billion with 4 per cent unemployment. But that is just the starting point for analysis and research to determine the proper demand stimulants and structural measures to attain our employment and growth.

The effectiveness of measures to expand consumer and investment demand depends heavily on the structural impediments to the flow of labor into available jobs. How far demand boosters can be pushed without touching off inflation depends heavily on the "fit" of the labor force in terms of skills and location to the jobs that expansion opens up. Thus the problem of structural unemployment—its size, nature, and trends—looms large in any discussion of aggregate demand policy.

Once structural unemployment is put in its rightful place, full employment policy has to define the demand deficiency it is tackling; that is, potential and actual demand must be measured and their anticipated course projected. Either now or later, is there, or will there be, enough demand in sight to meet our goals without fiscal and monetary stimuli?

If not, can we squeeze much additional demand out of shifts in the distributive shares? Again, if not, what does the Administration's current tax program offer by way of fiscal nourishment for a slack economy?

In the period of vigorous business activity in 1947 and 1948, the unemployment rate averaged 3.8 per cent of the labor force. After the recession of 1949 and the recovery of 1950, the rate remained approximately stable from early 1951 to late 1953, averaging 3.1 per cent. Thus, between 1947–1948 and 1951–1953, the unemployment rate fell by about one-fifth. Since that time, the rate has drifted upward. After the recession and recovery of 1953 and 1954, unemployment again stabilized from mid-1955 to late 1957. During this period the unemployment rate averaged about 4.2 per cent, an increase of more than one-third above the 1951–1953 period. Again, after the recession and recovery of 1957–1959, the unemployment rate stabilized briefly at a level of about 5.3 per cent in the first half of 1960—nearly one-fourth above the 1955–1957 level and more than two-thirds above the average for 1951–1953. After the recession and recovery of 1960–1961, the rate fluctuated within a narrow range, averaging 5.6 per cent in 1962.

No doubt the exceptionally low level of unemployment in 1951–1953 was partly a result of the fact that the economy was operating under forced draft during the Korean War. Although this was the one time since the Second World War during which an extended period of declining wholesale prices was experienced, it doubtless reflected the fact that speculative forces pushed many prices in 1950 and early 1951 above sustainable levels.

It has been the view of the Council of Economic Advisers that the rise in unemployment over recent years has been caused primarily by inadequate growth of aggregate demand. Accordingly, the primary line of attack on the twin problems of high unemployment and slow growth must be through measures, such as President Kennedy's program of tax reduction and reform, to speed the growth of total demand.

The Causes of Unemployment

There are two main views with respect to the causes of our present unemployment problem. The first is that the problem stems from lack of sufficient demand for labor to absorb all of those seeking work. According to this view, the primary solution to the problem lies in the adoption of monetary and fiscal policies which will expand total demand for goods and services, thus indirectly increasing the demand for labor.

The alternative thesis is that a fundamental cause of heavy unemployment is the appearance of serious imbalances in our labor markets associated with technological change, for example, automation, and with other structural changes which have altered the composition of demand for labor. According to this argument, in many cases the unemployed either (a) do not possess the proper training or ability to fill the jobs available, or (b) are not located where the vacancies exist, and are unable or unwilling to move, or (c) are unable to learn of the existence of suitable jobs. The problem, in other words, is primarily one of "square pegs" and "round holes." According to this view, a primary attack on the unemployment problem must be through the training and retraining of workers to raise their skill levels for available jobs, through measures to increase the geographical mobility of labor, and through efforts to increase the dissemination of information concerning job opportunities.

Many supporters of the structural unemployment thesis would probably accept the proposition that some autonomous stimulus to total demand is necessary if unemployment is to be reduced substantially, but they would insist that vigorous application of structural measures is also vital. At the same time, most of them apparently feel that structural measures by themselves without any autonomous demand stimulus can contribute importantly to the reduction of unemployment. On the other hand, most of those who would place the primary emphasis on demand creation would concede that such a policy could not reduce unemployment indefinitely without resort to structural measures. Nevertheless, there does exist a difference of opinion concerning the weights to be attached to demand creation on the one hand and structural adjustments on the other; in particular, there seems to be considerable skepticism in some circles as to whether expansion of aggregate demand by means of such measures as the Kennedy Administration's proposed program of tax reduction and reform is capable of making significant inroads on unemployment.

It is important to recognize at the outset that, even if the unemployment problem were primarily structural, a sufficient autonomous expansion of demand brought about by monetary or fiscal measures should be capable of melting it away. The expansion process would set up forces working on both the supply and demand sides of the economy which would work toward an improved matching of jobs and men. Occupations in which there were labor shortages would experience rapidly rising incomes, which would attract new workers entering the labor force, induce older workers to retrain themselves, and motivate employers to set up programs to train and retrain workers. Changes in relative wage rates would make more attractive those techniques which used labor that was readily available. Relatively lower prices of products utilizing ample labor supplies would induce shifts in demand, thus opening up jobs for less skilled workers. Labor shortages would generate increased recruiting efforts by employers, resulting in more widespread dissemination of job information. The appearance of premium wages would induce workers possessing the appropriate training and ability to relocate in areas where jobs were available. By these and other means, market adjustments would be generated by expanding demand and should reduce unemployment by an improved matching of men and jobs.

Indeed, in an economy in which prices and wages were flexible, this readaptation might come about as a result of declines in wages and prices in sectors and occupations having an excess supply of labor. But it is widely recognized that in the United States today prices and wages are much less flexible downward than upward. The result is that, while some adjustments may occur gradually through price and wage changes without an increase in total demand, rapid elimination of a serious mismatching of men and jobs would probably require an expansion of monetary demand. The adjustment would come primarily from an increase in wages and prices in those sectors and occupations suffering from labor shortages.

Thus, serious structural imbalances in labor markets do not signify that demand creation is incapable of reducing unemployment. But such imbalances would confront demand-creating policies with inflationary pressures much sooner than if unemployment is widely dispersed among occupations. In the latter case, the increased labor demands resulting from an expansionary policy can readily be met, with little need for relative price changes to readapt demand and supply in particular markets. In that event, the inflationary potential of demand creation will be minimal.[1]

Increase in Unemployment 1957–1962 by Occupation and Industry

Although the specter of structural, or technological, unemployment has often been raised in the past, it has recently taken on a new urgency related to the rise of "automation," and it is frequently invoked as a major explanation of the increase in unemployment that has occurred since 1957. One formulation of the structural unemployment thesis may be expressed as follows: In earlier periods technological change resulted in the specialization of function and division of labor. This simplification of the work process created many semiskilled and unskilled jobs. But, by contrast, in recent years further technological changes, including automation, have been reintegrating the production process and eliminating many semiskilled and unskilled jobs. The workers displaced in this way cannot fill either the jobs presently available or those created to increase aggregate demand.

If a substantial part of the increase in unemployment since 1957 were accounted for by this explanation, one would expect to find unusually large increases in unemployment (a) among blue-collar workers whose former jobs were vulnerable to displacement by automation, and (b) among goods-producing industries— mining, manufacturing, construction, transportation, and public utilities—which have so far experienced the most extensive automation. On the other hand, in professional, technical, and managerial occupations one would expect to find labor shortages, since workers in these fields would be capable of adapting to the increased demands of automation.

Over the entire postwar period, there does seem to be a decline in the rate of increase in *employment* in blue-collar occupations and goods-producing industries (see Table 1). But, when

TABLE 1. AVERAGE ANNUAL CHANGES IN EMPLOYMENT—
BLUE-COLLAR OCCUPATIONS AND GOODS-PRODUCING INDUSTRIES [a]
(Thousands)

Occupation or Industry	1948–53	1953–57	1957–62
Blue-collar occupations [b]	201	10	−97
Craftsmen, foremen, and kindred workers (skilled)	94	27	12
Operatives and kindred workers (semiskilled)	70	−29	−89
Laborers, except farm and mine (unskilled)	37	12	−20
Goods-producing industries [c]	425	−40	−230
Manufacturing	339	−94	−85
Mining	−26	−10	−36
Contract construction	91	75	−45
Transportation and public utilities	20	−12	−63

[a] Source: U. S. Department of Labor.
[b] Household survey data; data for 1957 and 1962 adjusted for comparability with prior data.
[c] Establishment data.

we examine the facts concerning changes in *unemployment rates* since 1957, we do not find much evidence of unusual behavior. Unemployment has risen by more than the average in some goods-producing industries and blue-collar occupations and by less than the average in others (see column 4 of Table 2). When all goods-producing industries are treated as a unit, the unemployment rate has risen by one percentage point, the same as for all other experienced wage and salary workers. When all blue-collar occupations are treated as a unit, the rate has risen by 1.4 percentage points, a larger than average increase.

However, this rise is not abnormal. We know that, when unemployment rises because of a deficiency in demand, the incidence of the increase is never evenly spread. Workers in higher skill categories are often "overhead" workers, who are kept on the payroll even when there is less need for their services. Goods-produc-

TABLE 2. Unemployment Rates in Industries and
Occupations Most Likely To Be Affected
by Automation, 1957–1962 [a]
(Per cent [b])

| | | | | Change in Rate | | |
| | | | | 1957–62 | | 1961– |
Industry or Occupation	1957	1961	1962	Ac-tual	Ex-pected [c]	62 Actual
All workers	4.3	6.7	5.6	1.3	—	−1.1
Experienced wage and salary workers	4.5	6.8	5.5	1.0	—	−1.3
Workers in selected industries (goods producing)	5.4	8.3	6.4	1.0	1.3	−1.9
Mining, forestry, and fisheries	6.3	11.6	8.6	2.3	1.8	−3.0
Construction	9.8	14.1	12.0	2.2	1.8	−2.1
Durable goods manufacturing	4.9	8.4	5.7	0.8	1.4	−2.7
Nondurable goods manufacturing	5.3	6.7	5.9	0.6	1.0	−0.8
Transportation and public utilities	3.1	5.1	3.9	0.8	1.0	−1.2
Experienced workers	3.9	5.9	4.9	1.0	—	−1.0
Workers in selected occupations (blue collar)	6.0	9.2	7.4	1.4	1.7	−1.8
Craftsmen, foremen, and kindred workers (skilled)	3.8	6.3	5.1	1.3	1.3	−1.2
Operatives and kindred workers (semiskilled)	6.3	9.6	7.5	1.2	1.6	−2.1
Laborers, except farm and mine (unskilled)	9.4	14.5	12.4	3.0	2.6	−2.1

[a] Sources: U. S. Department of Labor and Council of Economic Advisers.

[b] Per cent of civilian labor force in group.

[c] Calculated by use of correlations of (a) unemployment rates by industry with the rate for all experienced wage and salary workers, and (b) unemployment rates by occupation with the rate for all experienced workers, using data for the period of 1948–1957 in both cases.

ing industries are most cyclically sensitive, and hence workers are most adversely affected. Likewise unskilled and semiskilled workers are disproportionately affected both because of the industries in which most of them are employed and because of the vulnerability of persons in low skill categories. Therefore the rise in unemployment among blue-collar workers should be evaluated not only against the rise in the overall rate but also against the normal increase in unemployment that is to be expected when the overall unemployment rate increases. Our studies of the postwar relationships between unemployment in specific occupations and the overall unemployment rate for experienced workers show that, while for some the actual increase is greater than expected, in most cases it is less (see column 5 of Table 2). For all pertinent occupations and industries, taken together, the rise in unemployment is significantly less than would be expected.

Although the data seem to suggest a decline in structural unemployment since 1957 rather than a rise, it should be remembered that terminal year comparisons can be affected by a variety of erratic factors. The main conclusion to be drawn from the analysis is that changes in the overall unemployment rate explain most of the fluctuations in unemployment in the specific occupations and industries. Moreover, in general, the relationship between unemployment in these occupations and industries and the overall rate has not changed. If unemployment in blue-collar occupations and goods-producing industries is correlated with the overall unemployment rate and time for the postwar period, the partial correlation coefficient for the time trend is not significant, except for construction. In some instances—nondurable goods manufacturing and skilled workers—the trend coefficient is negative.[2]

Unemployment also increased substantially between 1957 and 1962 in service industries and in occupations other than blue collar (see column 4 of Table 3). In fact, unemployment has risen since 1957 in every major industry, including those with the most rapid rates of employment growth, and in every major occupation —excepting only farm owners—including those where labor is even now generally believed to be in short supply. The fact that the rise has been so widely dispersed can be attributed to the slackening of employment growth, to the high rate of interin-

TABLE 3. Unemployment Rates in Selected Industries
and Occupations, 1957–1962 [a]

(Per cent [b])

Industry or Occupation	1957	1961	1962	Change 1957–62 Ac-tual	Change 1957–62 Ex-pected [c]	1961–62 Actual
Selected industries						
Wholesale and retail trade	4.5	7.2	6.3	1.8	0.8	−0.9
Finance, insurance, and						
real estate	1.8	3.3	3.1	1.3	0.3	−0.2
Service industries	3.4	4.9	4.3	0.9	0.7	−0.6
Public administration	2.0	2.7	2.2	0.2	0.4	−0.5
Selected occupations						
Professional, technical,						
and kindred workers	1.2	2.0	1.7	0.5	0.3	−0.3
Managers, officials, and						
proprietors except farm	1.0	1.8	1.5	0.5	0.3	−0.3
Clerical and kindred						
workers	2.8	4.6	3.9	1.1	0.7	−0.7
Sales workers	2.6	4.7	4.1	1.5	0.5	−0.6
Private household workers	3.7	5.9	4.9	1.2	1.0	−1.0
Service workers, except						
private household	5.1	7.4	6.4	1.3	1.0	−1.0

[a] Sources: U. S. Department of Labor and Council of Economic Advisers.

[b] Per cent of civilian labor force in group.

[c] Calculated by use of correlations of (a) unemployment rates by industry with the rate for all experienced wage and salary workers, and (b) unemployment rates by occupation with rate for all experienced workers, using data for the period 1948–1957 in both cases.

dustry mobility, and to the fact that new entrants are increasingly attracted to white-collar occupations and service-producing industries.

The Distribution of Unemployment Reductions 1961–1962

The evidence presented above indicates little basis for the view that structural change contributed significantly to the increase in unemployment between 1957 and 1962. Further refutation of the structural unemployment thesis is provided by the changes that occurred between 1961 and 1962. The overall unemployment rate declined from 6.7 to 5.6, a drop of 16.4 per cent, as a result of an expansion of aggregate demand sufficient to produce a rise in GNP (valued at 1962 prices) of 5.4 per cent from $525.5 billion in 1961 to $553.9 billion in 1962. Unemployment declined substantially between 1961 and 1962 in the industries and occupations most likely to be unfavorably affected by structural factors (see the last column of Table 2). In some cases, indeed, the decline was substantially greater than the drop in the overall rate. Thus the unemployment rate fell by 3.0 points or 25.9 per cent in mining, by 2.7 points or 32.1 per cent in durable goods manufacturing, by 1.2 points or 23.5 per cent in transportation and public utilities, by 0.8 point or 19.0 per cent among craftsmen, and by 2.1 points or 21.9 per cent among operatives. In no case was the decline very much less than average.

Reductions in unemployment also occurred between 1961 and 1962 in all service industries and in all occupations other than blue collar (see the last column of Table 3). But, in relative terms, the declines in unemployment in these industries and occupations tended to be somewhat below average.

Thus the declines in unemployment associated with the expansion of aggregate demand between 1961 and 1962 were concentrated, if anywhere, in blue-collar occupations and goods-producing industries. This is what one would expect in view of the cycle sensitivity of many of these occupations and industries. But it does clearly demonstrate that structural maladjustments have not insulated whole categories of workers from the benefits of expanding demand.

It is true, as indicated earlier, that expansion of aggregate demand might reduce unemployment even in occupations afflicted with structural difficulties by bringing about demand-induced changes in relative wages and prices. Because of the downward inflexibility of wages and prices, this would mean a rise in overall average price and wage levels. If such adjustments took place, one would expect them in the form of increases in money wages exceeding the increases in labor productivity. However, between 1961 and 1962, on an economy-wide basis, the increase in hourly wages and salaries remained approximately in line with the 3.5

per cent increase in output per man-hour. And the wholesale price index rose by only 0.3 per cent between 1961 and 1962. That is, unemployment declined substantially in virtually every industry and occupation, and this decline occurred in a context of stable prices and noninflationary wage adjustments.

Job Vacancies and Unemployment

If unemployment had increased since 1957 because of structural imbalances rather than because of inadequacy of total demand, one would expect to observe an increase in unfilled job vacancies alongside the increase in unemployment. Of course, job vacancies could not be expected to increase as much as unemployment unless increased unemployment were entirely structural.[3] Nevertheless, some increase in job vacancies would presumably be expected. On the other hand, if the rise in unemployment were primarily caused by deficiency in aggregate demand, one would expect to observe a *decline* in job vacancies.

There is, of course, no comprehensive series specifically designed to measure unfilled job vacancies.[4] The National Industrial Conference Board, however, compiles an index based on the number of help-wanted ads published in a selected leading newspaper in each of 33 leading labor market areas. These areas account for 44 per cent of nonfarm employment.

The series is shown in Table 4 as published, and after adjust-

TABLE 4. INDEX OF HELP-WANTED ADVERTISEMENTS, 1955–1962 [a]

Year	Help-Wanted Index (1957 = 100)	Unemployment (thousands)	Help-Wanted Index—Civilian Labor Force (1957 = 100)	Unemployment Rate (per cent)
1955	100.7	2,904	103.9	4.4
1956	117.3	2,822	118.0	4.2
1957	100.0	2,936	100.0	4.3
1960	94.2	3,931	90.7	5.6
1962	100.1	4,012 [b]	94.4	5.6

[a] Sources: National Industrial Conference Board, U. S. Department of Labor, and Council of Economic Advisers.

[b] Adjusted by Council of Economic Advisers for comparability with prior data.

ment for changes in the size of the labor force. The adjusted series is the pertinent one, and it was actually lower in 1960 and 1962 than in 1955–1957. Thus the only available series indicates a decline in job vacancies since the last period when unemployment was at 4 per cent.[5]

Additional Comments on Structural Unemployment

The facts as presented and interpreted above strongly suggest that an expansion of aggregate demand can produce a significant reduction in unemployment without encountering structural imbalances in labor markets. They also suggest that expansion of aggregate demand is essential to reduction of unemployment; policies to improve labor market structure cannot do the job alone. But, as we look to the next few years, we must recognize that vigorous policies to deal with problems of labor market structure will be needed to complement our policies with respect to aggregate demand.

1. As unemployment melts away before expanding aggregate demand, we can expect problems of structural imbalances in particular labor markets to obstruct further expansion. If we are to succeed in reducing unemployment below our interim goal of 4 per cent, greater emphasis must be placed on structural policies designed to remove the obstacles of inadequate training and lack of mobility.

2. If we succeed in speeding up our rate of economic growth, we may well experience an associated increase in the pace of technological advance. This increase may lead to an accelerated rate of change of skill requirements, thereby increasing the need for structural measures to keep unemployment at minimum levels.

3. From 1963 to 1970, the number of young people entering the labor force is expected to average about 2.8 million per year, substantially above the average of 2.1 million per year between 1956 and 1962. The net increments to the labor force are expected to average about 1.3 million per year, compared with an average of about 800 thousand in 1956–1962.[6] Moreover, a large share of the new entrants to the labor force in the years ahead will be women and Negroes. Although it is not clear that specific unemployment rates by age, sex, or color have undergone systematic relative

changes in recent years, it is nevertheless true that unemployment rates for younger workers, for women, and for Negroes have remained consistently high. These high rates indicate the urgent need of efforts to improve the training of our young people. And they are another urgent reason, if another is needed, for the elimination of the roadblocks of discrimination because of color or sex.

The Inadequacy of Aggregate Demand

The foregoing analysis demonstrates that to cure our unemployment problem we must first expand aggregate demand. The next question is "How large is our deficiency in aggregate demand?" An answer to this question rests first on the level of our interim employment target, to be used in calculating the economy's near-term potentials.

As a starting point, we have used 4 per cent unemployment. We do not mean that the United States should settle for 4 per cent. As the Council of Economic Advisers stated in its 1963 *Annual Report* (p. 42),

Success in a combined policy of strengthening demand and adapting manpower supplies to evolving needs would enable us to achieve an interim objective of 4 per cent unemployment and permit us to push beyond it in a setting of reasonable price stability. Bottlenecks in skilled labor, middle-level manpower, and professional personnel tend to become acute as unemployment approaches 4 per cent. The result is to retard growth and generate wage-price pressures at particular points in the economy. As we widen or break these bottlenecks by intensified and flexible educational, training, and retraining efforts, our employment sights will steadily rise.

But reaching an interim goal, a way station, of 4 per cent would be no small achievement in itself.

To tie some employment magnitudes to this goal, it should be noted that 4 per cent unemployment by the end of 1963 adds up to an estimated increase of 3.1 million in employment over the level that prevailed at the end of 1962. Of these jobs, 1.2 million would be needed to absorb the normal increment in the labor force during 1963; 1.1 million would be needed to reduce unemployment from 5.5 to 4.0 per cent; and approximately another 800,000 would be needed to employ the workers who would be induced to enter, or re-enter, the labor force as a result of a resurgence of job opportunities. Total man-hours would grow even more than these figures suggest, what with longer weekly hours in tighter labor markets.

To achieve this increase in labor input would require a more than proportional increase in total output. New capital formation and technological change bring continuous productivity gains. More intensive utilization of existing capital facilities and already employed labor offer further increases in productivity.

Direct estimates of the relation between unemployment rates and output levels have been made; and the potential GNP has been independently estimated at 4 per cent unemployment. Both of these approaches yield consistent estimates of the output and demand requirements associated with the 4 per cent unemployment target at a given time. Subject to the customary modifications for cyclical variations in productivity and for temporary movements in labor force participation rates, it is estimated that every percentage point of unemployment above 4.0 per cent means a gap between actual and potential output of about 3.2 per cent of potential output. Thus, for 1962, when the unemployment rate averaged 5.6 per cent—1.6 percentage points above 4 per cent— and when participation rates were exceptionally low, the gap between potential and actual GNP was estimated at around $30 to $35 billion, or a little over 5 per cent of a potential $585 to $590 billion. Actually, the estimates of potential output (valued at constant prices) are very closely approximated by a 3½ per cent trend line passing through actual GNP in mid-1955.[7] By this trend line estimate, current dollar potential GNP was $586 billion in 1962, $32 billion above the actual level of $554 billion.

The trend line projection, allowing for an annual rate of increase of 1½ per cent in the GNP deflator, yields a potential GNP rate of $629 billion in the fourth quarter of 1963. This is over $65 billion, or nearly 12 per cent, above the level of $563.5 billion actually achieved in the last quarter of 1962. Thus it appears that an increase of some $65 billion in aggregate monetary demand would be needed to create the 3.1 million jobs that would reduce unemployment from the 5.5 per cent rate that prevailed in the fourth quarter of 1962 to the interim goal of 4.0 per cent by the fourth quarter of 1963. Allowing for the rise in potential output and a small increase in the GNP deflator, further increases in monetary demand of about 1¼ per cent, or between $7 and $8 billion per quarter, would be necessary in ensuing quarters to hold unemployment constant at 4 per cent.

In order to close the end-of-1962 output gap by the fourth quarter of 1963, GNP would have to rise an average of $16 billion in each quarter this year. The preliminary estimate of GNP for the the first quarter shows an $8.5 billion rise to a rate of $572 billion. This rise is a pleasant surprise to most forecasters—and is even a bit above the Kennedy Administration's expectations—but it is only slightly more than the advance needed just to hold the output gap constant.

To close the output gap by the end of 1964 would require average quarterly GNP increases of over $12 billion starting in 1963. With average quarterly gains no greater than the $8.5 billion registered in the first quarter of 1963, it would take roughly 10 years to erase the gap and reach 4 per cent unemployment.

Possible Solutions to the Problem of Deficient Demand

If there were natural forces at work in our economy which could be depended on to increase aggregate demand within a relatively short period of time, there might be reason for sitting tight. But unfortunately there are no such forces. It is true that over the longer pull there are demographic factors at work which may produce a substantial increase in demand. In due course, the large baby crop of the immediate postwar period will reach the age for marriage and household formation. When that happens we can hope for a spontaneous increase in the demand for homes, household appliances, automobiles, and all of the accoutrements of family living. However, not until the late 1960's and early 1970's will large numbers of children born in the immediate postwar period reach the age for marriage and the establishment of homes. Meanwhile, between 1962 and 1965, the midpoint of the Census Bureau estimates for the average annual increase in the number of households is 1.1 million per year, not greatly above the average increase of 1,022,000 per year that prevailed between 1957 and 1962.

We should also note that children born in the immediate postwar period will begin to enter the labor market very soon, typically some time before they reach the age for marriage and household formation. The need to provide them with adequate job opportunities thus precedes, both in priority and in timing, the need to accommodate their own latent demands.

It is plain, then, that action is needed to expand aggregate demand today. It is sometimes argued that this can be done by appropriately altering the distribution of income between wages and profits. But there is disagreement concerning the nature of the change that would be helpful: organized labor contends that wages should be increased in order to increase consumer purchasing power, while organized business says profits should be increased in order to stimulate investment. Most economists would agree that the impact of an income redistribution upon aggregate demand and employment is too complex and uncertain to be predicted in advance. More important, however, even if we knew the effects of income redistribution and were willing to ignore the ethical judgments implied, there is no reliable means by which wage and price policies could bring about an appreciable deliberate redistribution in a free society. If, for example, we encourage unions to seek increases in money wages which would increase labor's share of the national income, we have no means short of a strait-jacket wage and price controls to ensure that employers would not re-establish their share through higher product prices. Indeed, this would almost surely happen, thus doing untold harm to our balance of international payments without significantly expanding purchasing power, aggregate demand, and employment. Similarly, encouraging higher prices to stimulate investment would be likely to accelerate the rate of wage increases. An inflationary spiral without clear gain for real profits is the almost certain result.

Wage or price policies simply are not suitable vehicles for stimulating, or repressing, aggregate demand. They are more properly directed at assuring an environment of reasonable price stability within which an equitable sharing between labor and business of the fruits of economic progress can take place. This is the objective that the Kennedy Administration has sought to advance by means of the suggested guideposts for noninflationary wage and price adjustments.[8] Under the guideposts, wage increases would generally be kept within the limits of increased productivity so that the relative shares of national income going to labor and business would remain approximately constant.

An increase in aggregate demand is most appropriately brought about in a predominantly private-enterprise economy such as ours by means of monetary or fiscal measures. Under present conditions our balance-of-payments position contrains us from making full and vigorous use of expansionary monetary policy. It is necessary for us to keep our short-term interest rates reasonably aligned with those in foreign money centers in order to minimize outflows of short-term capital. Within the constraint imposed by this requirement, the Federal Reserve and the Treasury are conducting their current monetary and debt management operations in a way to avoid increases in long-term interest rates, and especially the sharp increases which occurred during the recovery of 1958–1960. Long-term rates are about as low now as they were at the cyclical turning point of February 1961. But the fact that the term structure of interest rates is strongly affected by the expectations of investors limits the ability of the monetary authorities to bring about lower long-term rates without permitting short-term rates to fall. It is doubtful whether much could be done beyond the actions that have already been taken to ease credit and reduce long-term rates while keeping short-term rates at the levels called for by balance-of-payments considerations.

With monetary policy thus constrained, we must concentrate on fiscal policy for expanding aggregate demand. In effecting an expansionary fiscal policy, we can work with the spending or the collecting sides of the federal budget. The Kennedy Administration has used both.

The administrative budget proposed for fiscal year 1964 calls for a $4½ billion increase in expenditures. The most significant increases are in the areas of defense and space. However, increases are also scheduled in a number of particularly important and productive civilian programs. Trust fund expenditures are rising by over $1 billion. And, within the framework of virtual stability in total administrative budget expenditures for other than defense, space, and interest, a $3.1 billion increase is actually scheduled for the most urgent civilian programs, with an offsetting decrease of $3.4 billion in expenditures of lower priority.

The largest decreases are projected for veterans' readjustment benefits, the United Nations loan, farm price supports, and the substitution of private for public credit—categories which together account for an expenditure reduction of $2.7 billion in the proposed budget.

Therefore present fiscal policies do provide for a share of our expanding productive resources to go for important public needs. Although at present the demands of our defense and space programs take the largest share of budget increases, important public domestic programs are expanding as well within the stable over-all total of civilian expenditures. In future years a larger share of budget increases can be expected to go toward the civilian programs that are necessary if we are to cope effectively with the problems and challenges of our society. But, in the current setting, larger increases in total expenditures than those scheduled do not seem the most acceptable and practicable method of providing additional fiscal stimulus to the economy. And additional stimulus is needed.

The kind of expenditure increases projected for this year and likely in subsequent years would prevent any significant increase in the fiscal drag on the economy. But they cannot be counted on to reduce that drag which prevails today. Therefore the deficiency in aggregate demand that now exists must be met by tax reduction aimed at increasing effective consumption and investment demands in the private sector.

The Kennedy Tax Program

The Kennedy Administration has recommended a comprehensive program of tax reduction and reform, to become effective in stages over a period of 18 months. As proposed by President Kennedy, the first stage of this program would by July 1, 1963, lower the net tax liabilities of consumers and business by roughly $6 billion at an annual rate.

When the full program is in effect on January 1, 1965, the net reduction in annual tax liabilities after reforms would be well in excess of $10 billion a year, on the basis of 1963 levels of income. More than $8 billion of the reductions would be in individual income taxes with the cut in corporate income tax liabilities accounting for the remainder.

The Kennedy program contains path-breaking boldness. Its dual objective is to restore aggregate demand to full employment levels and to improve the incentives for private initiative that will accelerate economic growth in the long run. Never before has a President built his fiscal policies so clearly, so deliberately, and so thoroughly to meet the needs of the economy for an expansionary stimulus. This is surely a milestone in the history of U. S. economic policy under the Employment Act of 1946.

President Kennedy has proposed to give the economy a deliberate fiscal stimulus in spite of public and Congressional concern about budget deficits and public debt. Substantial tax reduction is proposed at a time when an increase of roughly $5 billion in federal expenditures is also being recommended and the short-run budget outlook already includes a substantial deficit. The Kennedy Administration realizes that economic expansion and full employment are the objectives of first priority, and that in any case the chances of balancing the federal budget are poor except in a growing and fully operating economy.

Nor is the tax reduction proposal based on a simply antirecession precaution. We are not in recession, and latest readings lend impressive strength to the forecast in the 1963 *Economic Report* that no recession will occur in 1963. Fears of recession always lurk in the background in an economy which has had four recessions since the Second World War. And the tax program provides important insurance against recession during its phasing-in period, in particular. But our basic problem is more subtle than recession and at the same time more deep-seated. The economy has been expanding; but for some time the pace of expansion has not been rapid enough to narrow the gap that exists between our actual output and our productive potential. As a result, the unemployment rate has remained unacceptably high.

The tax program will set in motion a number of interacting sets of stimuli to increase output and employment: [9]

1. When the full $10 billion of tax reduction is in effect, it will increase disposable personal income by about $8½ billion per year. This calculation is for the 1963 tax base, and it includes both the reductions in individual income taxes and the additional dividends generated by corporate tax reduction. Assuming that consumption increases by about 93 per cent of the rise in disposable income—the ratio has consistently ranged between 92 and 94 per cent in recent years—personal consumption expenditures

will increase by about $8 billion per year. As output is adjusted to the increased demand, production and income will also rise by $8 billion per year. Allowing for the various leakages—federal tax collections (at the new lower tax rates), state and local taxes, and corporate and personal saving—which according to estimates will absorb about 50 per cent of the rise in gross income, the remaining 50 per cent of the initial increase in GNP will find its way back into personal consumption and stimulate further production and income. When the entire cycle of successive rounds of income and consumption has worked its way through the system, it should raise income by roughly $16 billion, about half of the present gap. Thus it is estimated that the pure consumption multiplier applicable to the entire tax cut, personal and corporate, is about 1.6.

Some observers have worried aloud whether the stimulus of federal tax reduction may not be in part offset by increases in state and local taxes. The theory is that tax collectors abhor a vacuum. The fact is that the expenditures of many state and local governments are up against the limit set by their financial resources. If federal tax reduction permits them to increase their revenues, whether through higher tax rates or expansion of their tax base, it will equally permit them to increase their expenditures. The aggregate demand stimulus will be the same whether the federal tax savings are spent directly by the taxpayers or indirectly, at their command, by their state and local governments. The pressing needs for the public facilities and services provided by these governments suggest that, if federal tax reduction can improve the financial situation of these governments, this improvement should be considered a benefit of the program rather than a defect.

2. The increased sales of consumer goods will raise business profits and internal funds, and the increased production will reduce margins of excess capacity in industry. For both these reasons, business investment will be stimulated. The importance of a general increase in demand and in visible business markets for revitalizing private investment should be stressed. Business investment has been at disappointingly low levels in 1958–1962. Indeed, gross private domestic investment is the one major component of economic activity which has shown no upward trend since the mid-1950's. It did not return to its 1955 peak of $75 billion (in

1962 prices) until 1962 when real GNP had risen by 21 per cent. Fixed investment in relation to GNP has fallen from the 10 to 11 per cent levels of the 1949–1957 period to an average of only 9 per cent in 1958–1962. The existing stock of business plant and equipment has increased by only 2 per cent a year since 1957, compared with 4 per cent a year in the 1947–1957 period. And 1962 was the first nonrecession year in the postwar period when corporate investment fell short of corporate saving.

Therefore a major objective of expansionary policy is to increase investment. This is the reason for the changes in business taxation which the Kennedy Administration has already adopted and for the reductions in the corporate tax rate now proposed. But they cannot do the job alone. Investment cannot be lifted by its own bootstraps. A substantial general improvement in sales and expected sales through major income tax reduction must be coupled with direct investment incentives if businessmen are to undertake large-scale commitments to new capacity.

3. The reduction in business tax rates—particularly the corporate rate—will also serve both to increase business cash flow and to raise the prospective profitability of new investment. And the tax inducements put into effect in 1962—more liberal depreciation allowances and the 7 per cent investment tax credit—will work to stimulate investment still further. Indeed, these measures will be increasingly powerful as final demand expands and excess capacity shrinks.

4. The increased investment resulting from (2) and (3) above will generate further increases in consumption via the multiplier.

The investment response is difficult to estimate precisely. But it is believed that the program offers a good prospect of getting the American economy moving steadily toward full employment. Recent improvements in the outlook suggest that the tax reduction will be operating from a stronger base. Even so, it will take time to eliminate the slack that has developed in the course of five years of subnormal economic activity. But, as soon as the program is enacted, it will provide a sizable and growing stimulus. Unemployment rates should then begin to drop fairly quickly. There is a good prospect that after the full program is in operation unemployment will move down to 4 per cent. It will then be our challenge to prove that 4 per cent is too modest a goal.

NOTES

1. It should, of course, be recognized that the absence of serious structural imbalances in the labor market—or the adoption of adequate measures to deal with them—is not sufficient in itself to ensure that inflation will be avoided in the process of reducing unemployment. Even in the absence of structural difficulties, the exercise of market power by large companies or large labor organizations or both can be a source of inflationary difficulties during a period of declining unemployment. The wage-price guideposts set forth by the Council of Economic Advisers in its *Annual Report* for 1962 (pp. 185–190) and reaffirmed in its *Annual Report* for 1963 (pp. 85–86) are aimed primarily at this problem. In addition, bottlenecks could arise in particular industries as a result of capital shortages; at the present time, however, the existence of widespread excess plant capacity suggests that this problem is not likely to be a significant one.

2. As a final check, the unemployment rate in blue-collar occupations and goods-producing industries was correlated with the overall rate and with a "discontinuity variable" which shifted values after 1957. The discontinuity variable was not a significant explanatory factor, except for construction. In other words, there is no evidence of any change in relationship after 1957.

3. Even in this case, the rise in vacancies and the rise in unemployment would not be identical—one does not hire a secretary unless he can hire the professional person for whom she will work.

4. One of the recommendations of the President's Committee to Appraise Employment and Unemployment Statistics, headed by Professor R. A. Gordon, was that the federal government should develop such a series, and funds have been provided for this purpose in the federal budget for the fiscal year 1964.

5. It should be noted that the vacancies-unemployment balance is somewhat sensitive to cyclical movements, with vacancies rising relative to unemployment in periods of expansion and falling relative to unemployment in periods when the pace of activity is slowing down. Thus the 1960–1962 rise in vacancies in relation to unemployment is normal, as was the 1956–1957 decline, and not evidence of structural change.

6. This comparison may in a sense overstate the magnitude of our problem during the remainder of the 1960's relative to 1956–1962, since labor force participation rates were depressed during that period by the lack of available jobs. In order to have maintained continuing full employment in 1956–1962, in other words, we would have had to provide more than 800,000 additional jobs per year.

7. For a full discussion of the estimates of potential output and the gap, see "The American Economy in 1961: Problems and Policies," Statement of the Council of Economic Advisers, *January 1961 Economic Report of the President and the Economic Situation and Outlook,* Hearings Before the Joint Economic Committee, 87th Cong., 1st sess., February, March, and

April 1961, pp. 321–329, and Supplement A, pp. 373–377; also A. M. Okun, "Potential GNP: Its Measurement and Significance," Cowles Foundation Paper No. 190 (1963), reprinted from the 1962 *Proceedings of the Economic Statistics Section of the American Statistical Association*.

8. See the Annual Reports of the Council of Economic Advisers for 1962 (pp. 185–190) and 1963 (pp. 85–86).

9. For a fuller discussion of the "multiplier" and "accelerator" effects of the tax program, see the 1963 *Annual Report* of the Council of Economic Advisers, pp. 45–51; and the Council's statement to the Joint Economic Committee in *January 1963 Economic Report of the President*, Hearings Before the Joint Economic Committee, 88th Cong., 1st sess., January and February, 1963, pp. 1–18, 24–25 (see especially Chart 1, p. 13, Chart 2, p. 14, and Chart 3, p. 25, which give a graphic view of the expansion process).

CHAPTER 5

Aggregate Demand and the Current Unemployment Problem

BY OTTO ECKSTEIN

This chapter deals with the relation between aggregate demand and unemployment. Five questions are considered: First, is there an unemployment problem or is it all statistical illusion? Second, if there is an increase in unemployment, can it be explained by structural or regional peculiarities of the labor force? Third, are there relationships between movements in the Gross National Product and unemployment? Fourth, what is the outlook for aggregate demand in the coming year or two; and, if the economy is to return to full employment, will our present labor force meet the job requirements? Fifth, which unemployment problems will an increase of aggregate demand fail to solve? In dealing with these questions, some of the empirical evidence that can be brought to bear will be reviewed. Since the Berkeley program is now in its early stages and represents one of the most massive applications of scientific resources to the solution of this problem, let us identify some areas of our ignorance which may yield to research.

There Is an Unemployment Problem

The unemployment problem is not a statistical illusion. The national unemployment rate has averaged 6 per cent for the 1958–1962 period and has not been below 5 per cent in the last 65 months. This level compares with an average rate of 4.2 per cent for the earlier postwar period, 1946–1957, even though the earlier period also contained two recessions. Perhaps more alarming is the increase in unemployment in "good times." In 1947–1948 this rate was 3.8 per cent; in 1951–1953, 3.1 per cent; in 1955–1957, 4.3 per cent; in 1959–1960, 5.5 per cent; and in the current recovery, 5.5 to 6.0 per cent. Nor is there serious reason to question the accuracy and meaningfulness of these annual figures. The Gordon Report to President Kennedy [1] found that "The concept of unemployment now in official use is a reasonable one and represents a conscientious and well designed effort over a long period of time to resolve a wide range of difficult issues." This report leaves no doubt that unemployment is being measured properly, and that the increase of recent years is a reality.

Further evidence can be found in the international comparisons of Kalachek and Westebbe [2] and of the Gordon Report. European figures are substantially lower than our own, but the methods of measurement are not the same. Kalachek and Westebbe found that the difference in unemployment figures in good times due to conceptual differences between the British and American figures may be a maximum of 1.5 per cent, which is much smaller than the actual difference in the figures of recent years. The United Kingdom's greater sensitivity to unemployment can be seen in the recent riots of unemployed workers before Parliament at unemployment rates much below ours. The comparisons for eight countries in the Gordon Report [3] are even more striking. They show that, if the European figures are put on the same conceptual basis as our own, the 1960 rates for France, Germany, Japan, and Sweden were between 1 and 2 per cent, for Great Britain 2.4 per cent, and for Italy 4.3 per cent. Only Canada, which is heavily dependent on our own economy, suffered from a higher unemployment rate, 7.0 per cent.

What fraction of our unemployment can be attributed to frictional factors? The Bureau of Labor Statistics [4] has estimated that during the 1955–1957 period frictional unemployment accounted for about 20 per cent of the then unemployed—or 0.9 per cent of the labor force; voluntary job shifting accounted for another 10 per cent—or 0.4 per cent of the labor force—excluding new job seekers, or another 25 per cent—1.1 per cent—if they are included; seasonal unemployment represented another 20 per cent—0.9 per cent of the labor force. All in all, short-term frictional factors accounted for unemployment representing only 2.5 per cent of the labor force. The Bureau of Labor Statistics foresaw a rise of 0.5 per cent in frictional unemployment by 1975 due to coming demographic changes, including more younger and older workers. Thus 3.0 per cent is a liberal estimate of frictional unemployment under current conditions. The remainder is due to general unemployment and longer-term structural elements, particularly the rise of unemployment in goods-producing industries.

This figure, 3.0 per cent, is much smaller than the interim target, 4.0 per cent, which the Council of Economic Advisers has endorsed. The Council of Economic Advisers has selected 4.0 per cent on the ground that it is consistent with price level stability.[5] It does not seem that the full employment objective should be defined in terms of its compatibility with another objective. Perhaps, with the present structure of the economy, full employment is inconsistent with stable prices; perhaps not. But it seems to be implicit theorizing to achieve compatibility of the objectives by lowering one's goals until compatibility is achieved by definition. If new policies are needed to achieve genuine compatibility, let us consider them on their own merits.

What, then, is a reasonable definition of full employment? It is impossible to define an absolute target rate of unemployment, since both normal short-term frictional unemployment and the additional unemployment which permits long-term structural adjustments of the growing labor force vary over time. However, in light of the experience in other advanced economies, which have enjoyed unemployment rates between 0 and 2 per cent, as well as our unemployment experience during earlier periods of prosperity, it is difficult to envisage the development of widespread labor shortages while our unemployment was near the 4 per cent level.

Unemployment in 1958–1962, therefore, has been above a normal level by more than 2 per cent. The resultant loss of output is substantially greater because of the resultant decline in the growth of the labor force, the retardation of productivity, and the induced decline in investment.

The study by the Bureau of Labor Statistics on which this discussion was based covered the period 1955–1957. It is a research task of high priority to bring this study up to date,[6] and to develop further the underlying concepts of the major structural components of unemployment.

Is the Rise in Unemployment Structural?

A few years ago the view was widely held that the increase in unemployment was due to structural peculiarities of the economy. The skillful and elaborate study by Kalachek and Knowles [7] has shown that there has been no increased dispersion of unemployment by skill or by industry, and that unemployment cannot be explained by any acceleration of productivity trends or by decreased worker mobility. Attention should be directed to the comparisons of unemployment in 1957 and 1962 in the President's Manpower Report. These figures show substantial and relatively even increases in the unemployment rates of all groups of workers, whether arranged by sex, by age, by major occupation group, by race, by industry, or almost any combination of these classifications.

The regional distribution of unemployment is another aspect of the problem. Unemployment has become more evenly diffused through the economy in recent years. Unpublished studies by Denison [8] present a comparison of unemployment rates among states and among metropolitan areas for the years 1950 and 1960, using data from the Census of Population. These studies show a marked change toward a greater uniformity of unemployment rates.

Some additional computations have been performed, using the data for 150 major labor market areas in the President's Manpower Report. Table 1 compares the distribution of unemployment among areas according to their unemployment rate. Let us compare 1959, 1960, and 1962, three years with almost identical national unemployment rates. By 1962, fewer areas had ex-

TABLE 1. Distribution of Unemployment in 150 Major Labor
Market Areas of the United States, 1959, 1960, 1962

Percentage of Unemployment	Number of Areas			Number of Persons (thousands)			Percentage of Total for 150 Areas		
	1959	1960	1962	1959	1960	1962	1959	1960	1962
16 or more	1	—	—	14.8	—	—	0.59	—	—
14.0–15.9	2	—	1	32.0	—	13.1	1.28	—	0.54
12.0–13.9	4	4	3	31.1	52.0	17.0	1.24	2.15	0.71
10.0–11.9	4	4	4	51.4	24.5	39.4	2.05	1.01	1.63
8.0– 9.9	11	11	6	379.5	165.0	126.4	15.14	6.81	5.24
6.0– 7.9	30	39	32	441.0	644.8	579.7	17.60	26.61	24.04
4.0– 5.9	60	67	73	1,327.3	1,370.5	1,407.4	52.96	58.57	58.36
2.0– 3.9	38	25	31	229.1	166.0	228.4	9.14	6.85	9.47
0 – 1.9	—	—	—	—	—	—	—	—	—
Total	150	150	150	2,506.2	2,422.8	2,411.4	100.00	100.00	100.00

treme values of unemployment; for example, in 1959 twenty-two
areas had unemployment above 8 per cent, in 1962 only fourteen.
Also, fewer of the unemployed were in the extreme areas, 20 per
cent in areas with unemployment above 8 per cent in 1959, 8
per cent in 1962.

Comparing the ranks of these major labor market areas by their
unemployment rates also showed some interesting changes. Of
eleven areas which suffered from unemployment in excess of 10
per cent in 1959, there was important improvement in six of them,
including at least one case of complete cure. Of the ten areas with
unemployment below 3 per cent in 1959, only two remained in
that happy state three years later.

One phenomenon still requires explanation. The total unemployment in these 150 labor market areas has represented a declining fraction of the total national unemployment, as can be
seen from Table 2. Since unemployment rates for farm labor declined between 1958 and 1962, the location of the increase of unemployment outside the 150 major labor market areas is not at all
clear. Perhaps the difference is in measurement techniques.

In order to cover a longer period, figures are also presented for
1950 to 1962 for insured unemployment for the 50 states (see

TABLE 2. ANALYSIS OF UNEMPLOYMENT IN 150 MAJOR
LABOR MARKET AREAS FOR 1958–1962

Year	Total Unemployment in 150 Areas (thousands)	Total in U.S. (thousands)	Total in 150 Areas as % of U.S. Total
1958	3,204.7 a	4,681	68.462
1959	2,506.2	3,813	65.728
1960	2,422.8	3,931	61.633
1962	2,411.4	4,007	60.180

a Figures available for only 147 areas.

Table 3). This omits some important categories of the unemployed, particularly workers in agriculture, domestic service, nonprofit organization, unpaid family, and self-employed workers, and most state and local government employees; however, the figures are particularly reliable since they are based on comprehensive accounting records. The dispersion of unemployment rates, as measured by the standard deviation, was lower in 1962 than earlier, and this result is even more striking in terms of the coefficient of variation. The data also indicate considerable change in rankings over the years. The New England States loomed large among the depressed areas of the early 1950's, and their unemployment rates have fallen significantly. The problem areas of our own day, West Virginia and Pennsylvania, were prosperous in 1956, and by 1962 already showed a significant improvement as compared with 1959. Thus there is a good deal of change and adjustment going on in the economy. Depressed areas do not stay depressed forever, and one must recognize that "structural" does not always mean "permanent."

It is therefore concluded that the persistently high level of unemployment in the 1958–1962 period is not due to structural peculiarities but is generally diffused into all broad sectors of the economy. This is not to deny that unemployment has structure, that this structure deserves intensive study, and that some components of unemployment will yield to increased general prosperity more readily than others.

TABLE 3. INSURED UNEMPLOYMENT IN 50 STATES AND
DISTRICT OF COLUMBIA, SELECTED YEARS 1950–1962,
BY RANK IN 1962 AND 1950

State	Rates of Insured Unemployment for					Ranking	
	1962	1959	1956	1952	1950	1962	1950
Alaska	10.8	12.5	8.2	6.8	7.3	1	3
W. Va.	6.8	8.3	3.2	4.3	5.3	2	15
Pa.	6.3	6.8	4.4	3.2	3.9	3	29.5
Wash.	6.0	5.9	4.7	4.2	6.5	4	8
Ark.	5.9	5.6	4.6	3.7	5.6	5	11
Ky.	5.7	6.1	6.7	4.3	5.2	6	16.5
Maine	5.5	7.3	4.4	4.5	8.3	7	2
Calif.	5.4	4.1	2.6	3.3	6.9	8	5
Tenn.	5.3	5.1	5.9	4.6	6.0	9	10
N.J.	5.2	5.5	4.5	3.2	5.0	10.5	19
N. Dak.	5.2	4.8	3.9	2.9	4.0	10.5	26
Alabama	5.0	5.2	4.2	3.7	5.1	13	18
Miss.	5.0	5.2	5.0	4.6	6.1	13	9
R.I.	5.0	5.5	5.1	6.6	7.2	13	4
Idaho	4.9	4.6	3.7	3.1	4.9	17	20.5
La.	4.9	4.6	2.3	3.1	4.9	17	20.5
Mass.	4.9	4.5	2.8	3.8	5.4	17	13.5
Mont.	4.9	6.7	3.1	2.4	5.2	5	16.5
Oregon	4.9	4.6	4.6	4.5	6.7	17	6
N.Y.	4.8	5.2	3.5	3.8	6.6	21	7
Vt.	4.8	4.2	2.7	3.9	5.4	21	13.5
Wyo.	4.8	3.4	2.4	1.0	2.7	21	41
Mich.	4.5	5.3	5.3	3.2	2.9	23.5	40
Okla.	4.5	4.1	2.9	2.7	4.7	23.5	23
Md.	4.4	5.0	1.8	1.8	3.6	25	34
Nev.	4.2	4.9	4.2	2.2	5.5	26.5	12
Ohio	4.2	3.1	1.9	1.5	3.5	26.5	35.5
Minn	4.0	3.9	3.2	2.4	3.5	29	35.5
Mo.	4.0	3.6	3.1	2.1	3.9	29	29.5
N.M.	4.0	2.7	2.0	1.4	2.5	29	42.5
Ariz.	3.9	3.9	2.6	1.7	3.9	31.5	29.5
Hawaii	3.9	2.6	3.0	3.0	4.3	31.5	24
Fla.	3.8	3.2	2.5	2.5	3.9	33.5	29.5

TABLE 3. *Continued*

State	Rates of Insured Unemployment for					Ranking	
	1962	1956	1956	1952	1950	1962	1950
N.C.	3.8	4.1	3.9	3.5	4.0	33.5	26
Conn.	3.5	4.4	2.3	1.9	3.8	35.5	32
N.H.	3.5	4.1	4.5	5.2	8.5	35.5	1
Del.	3.4	3.3	1.6	1.1	2.1	37.5	47
Ga.	3.4	3.8	3.2	2.4	3.3	37.5	37
Utah	3.3	3.4	2.3	2.1	3.7	39	33
Ill.	3.2	3.3	2.3	2.6	4.8	40.5	22
Ind.	3.2	3.1	2.9	2.1	2.1	40.5	47
S.C.	3.1	3.3	3.4	2.6	4.0	42	26
Wis.	3.0	2.7	2.3	1.7	2.0	43	49
Col.	2.9	2.2	1.3	0.7	2.3	44	44
Kan.	2.8	2.7	2.3	1.2	3.0	45.5	38.5
Texas	2.8	2.8	1.4	0.9	1.8	45.5	51
S. Dak.	2.7	2.1	2.6	1.5	2.5	47	42.5
Iowa	2.5	1.9	2.0	1.5	2.1	48.5	47
Nebraska	2.5	2.0	2.5	1.2	2.2	48.5	45
Va.	2.1	2.6	1.8	1.7	3.0	50	38.5
D.C.	2.0	1.9	1.7	0.9	1.9	51	50
National average	4.4	4.4	3.2	2.9	4.6		
Standard deviations of rates	1.452	1.853	1.409	1.407	1.725		
Coefficient of variations	0.3349	0.4263	0.4244	0.4822	0.3936		

Relationships between Changes in Gross National Product and Unemployment

That the national unemployment rate is mainly a product of the aggregate movements of the economy is thus strongly borne out by the statistics. So far, no independent large-scale effort has been made to explain the unemployment rate in terms of other economic variables. However, various econometric model-building efforts have included unemployment equations whose accuracy is as reliable as other macro-economic relations. The Michigan model of Suits,[9] the Klein-Goldberger model,[10] the recent model of Gary Fromm,[11] as well as my own efforts with Duesenberry and Fromm,[12] contain such equations. This is not the proper time to review them all.

The following is a crude equation which has been used in recent years to predict unemployment.

Annual rate of change of unemployment $= 0.3$ (3.5%—the annual rate of growth of real GNP)

This equation says that unemployment will remain constant if the real rate of growth is 3.5 per cent, that it improves by 0.3 per cent for every 1 per cent of GNP growth above the long-term 3.5 per cent trend level, and that it worsens in a symmetrical manner. According to this simple equation, to reach full employment in two years would require a real growth rate of 6.8 per cent a year, while over four years it would require a growth rate of 5.2 per cent. Thus, if this equation is correct, it would indeed be difficult to return to 4 per cent unemployment, and it would require substantial growth in excess of 3.5 per cent per year.

The equation is derived, not from short-term time series, but strictly from changes in output and unemployment between business cycle peaks. Figure 1 shows the postwar observations, including the current one. The peak-to-peak approach was used because it was desirable to abstract from cyclical swings in unemployment. This approach seriously restricts the number of observations, but for a long-term analysis it is more meaningful to derive the parameters from these data than to base them on short-term cyclical swings. A cursory examination of the prewar data suggests that the formula is not so readily applicable. Nor is the possibility excluded that a nonlinear relationship is involved.

In some respects the relationship is too simple. In particular, it makes the rate of unemployment independent of population movements which affect the growth of the labor supply. The good fit seems to be due to the fact that the growth of the labor force responds to the growth of demand for labor, so that the effect of demographic swings on unemployment is very much attenuated.

These notes are just a beginning on this problem. Obviously,

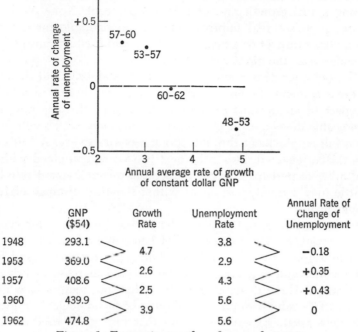

	GNP ($54)	Growth Rate	Unemployment Rate	Annual Rate of Change of Unemployment
1948	293.1		3.8	
		4.7		−0.18
1953	369.0		2.9	
		2.6		+0.35
1957	408.6		4.3	
		2.5		+0.43
1960	439.9		5.6	
		3.9		0
1962	474.8		5.6	

Figure 1. Economic growth and unemployment.

statistical explanations of unemployment rates in different regions and different industries still have to be undertaken. A more complete econometric theory of the structure of unemployment would also explain (1) the participation rates which determine the labor force, (2) the work week, and (3) the demand for labor based on a theory of productivity growth.

The Outlook for Aggregate Demand and Aggregate Unemployment

We shall not present a long-term forecast of unemployment over the next five or ten years, but let us examine the current consensus on the short-term outlook. Forecasting experts, both inside and outside the government, now expect that the total growth of output in the current period will be at about the rate of 3 per cent. After the recent brightening in the business outlook, the optimists are projecting GNP figures reflecting an implicit real growth rate of about 3.5 to 4.0 per cent. The pessimists are projecting a real growth rate of 2.5 to 3 per cent. None of these figures promises real improvement in the unemployment rate. With little prospect of a tax cut having a major effect during this calendar year, the die is cast for 1963.

The behavior of unemployment in 1964 and 1965 will depend on the enactment of a tax cut. Without a tax cut there is now little prospect of an upward breakthrough; that is, there is now no foreseeable development in the private economy which will produce full employment through spontaneous recovery. A $10 billion tax cut enacted during the next two years, combined with a multiplier of perhaps 2 might reduce the unemployment rate by a little over 1 point, putting us within shooting distance of full employment.[13]

In the later years of the 1960's the outlook for the private economy is brighter. The higher rate of household formation should lead to a greater volume of house building, greater demand for automobiles and appliances, and an induced increase in private investment. These demands are channeled into sectors in which productivity is high and the possibilities of technological progress relatively great. Experience shows that prosperity in these industries is an essential ingredient for high general economic growth. On the other side, the growth of the working population also accelerates, so that more expansion is necessary to provide jobs.

It would be a mistake to place excessive faith in the expected favorable demographic developments alone. If the economy is kept below full employment and full capacity utilization year after year, the economic potential of these developments may well be frustrated. A changing age structure of the population does not automatically convert itself into demand for final product or requirements for additional capital. The resultant changes in the marginal propensity to consume are limited, and if household incomes do not rise at a sufficient rate neither will the final demands. Family formation itself is affected by economic conditions, as marriages are postponed when there is unemployment; demands for houses can become demands for apartments or even doubling up with in-laws. The outlook for the late 1960's offers little argument for the postponement of the necessary tax changes.

Structural Changes in the Composition
of Full Employment Demand

If the return to full employment follows the path indicated above, there seems to be no reason to anticipate structural impediments. On the whole, this resurgence of demand in the durable goods industries and construction would be a stimulus to employment where the decline has been felt most acutely in 1957–1962. Similarly, the balanced tax cut proposed by President Kennedy, designed to stimulate both consumption and investment, would lead to a diffused increase of demand for all sectors of the economy which would create few shortages.

These assertions are based only on the crudest analysis, and it would clearly be desirable to make elaborate sectoral projections of the growth of demand and employment for the remainder of this decade. It would also be useful to identify future shortages of specific skills as well as the coming geographic pattern of expansion. The Government's Interagency Growth Study should provide useful information along these lines.

What Unemployment Problems Will Aggregate
Demand Increases Fail to Solve?

From what has been said so far, we might think that stimulation of the economy through fiscal methods will eliminate unemployment in its entirety. This is obviously incorrect. The preceding discussion was presented because it is too easy to get carried away by the extreme cases, particularly the plight of West Virginia coal miners. The case approach, as exemplified in an interesting issue of *Newsweek* magazine,[14] makes us lose sight of the basic fact that only an increase in aggregate demand is capable of reducing aggregate unemployment by a substantial amount. We can turn to the structural aspects of the problem only when we see it in terms of the economy as a whole. Stubborn problems will remain even after aggregate demand has been restored to an optimal level. In addition to the structural measures already taken, chiefly the Area Redevelopment Act and the Manpower Development and Training Act, further steps will be necessary before our society can feel content that it has taken sufficient action to deal with one of the most acute domestic problems throughout our industrial history.

From a social point of view, not all unemployment is equally serious. The teenager casually attached to the labor force, the housewife who is the second or third labor force member of her household, the worker contentedly collecting his unemployment benefits in Florida during the off-season should cause us less worry than the unemployed head of a household who has been out of a job for more than six months.[15] Let us now turn to the problems that will remain even when aggregate demand has been restored to a level consistent with aggregate supply.

The Six Special Groups with a Particularly High Incidence of Unemployment

The President's Manpower Report has identified six groups with the highest incidence of unemployment; we shall examine each of them in turn.

Young workers. Unemployment in this group is always high, although from 1957 to 1962 it crept up a few per cent, in line with the increased unemployment for all other age groups. In the coming years the number of new entrants to the labor force will increase further. The high unemployment rate of this group is largely due to frequent job shifting as young people experiment with different careers, to a lack of economic responsibilities which gives them the freedom to quit a job, and, in some cases, to the lack of skill and seniority.

This group's unemployment rate may well return to normal, if rather high, levels when general full employment is restored. The group is mobile, adaptable, and responsive to changing skill needs. When job opportunities are abundant in any field, young people will adapt their training and will seek them out. They pose a special problem for the next few years because their numbers rise so rapidly.

The high youth unemployment rate partly reflects the inadequacies of our school system. The high school dropouts are the most serious hard-core unemployed of the group. Their plight is due to two factors, neither of which is amenable to quick solution: First, inappropriate school curricula offer only academic courses to students who lack the capacity or the interest to absorb such material; no vocational training is provided in which the student might see some positive benefit.[16] Second, many dropouts are not work-oriented, and hence their integration into the economic system is very difficult. Frequently they come from environments characterized by acute social disorganization. What should properly be done for this group is far beyond my expertise; dropping out of school and being unemployed are usually only symptoms of a larger problem to which our society does not seem to have found the answer.

Older workers. Workers over 45 do not have particularly high unemployment rates—4.0 per cent in 1962—but a larger percentage remain unemployed for 15 weeks or longer. Of all males in the labor force in the age bracket 45–64, some 1.6 per cent were unemployed for 15 weeks or more in 1962. Since the bulk of these men are heads of households, they constitute a particularly important group of the unemployed. A return to full employment would be beneficial: in 1957, only 0.9 per cent of this group suffered from long-term unemployment.

The United States has always been ruthless with the older worker, and re-employment has been difficult for him. The higher long-term unemployment rate of the older workers of the last few years is a by-product of the decline of certain industries, particularly the goods-producing industries and some branches of mining.[17]

Negro workers. Unemployment rates for nonwhite workers have been more than twice as high as the rates for white workers, and, to the extent that a trend is discernible, their relative position has been worsening through most of the postwar period. While new fields have slowly opened for Negroes, they still remain most vulnerable when unemployment comes. Negroes have a particularly large stake in a return to full employment, since their unemployment will decrease by an extremely large amount.

The longer-term problem of bringing Negro unemployment rates down to the national average level is very complex. The higher unemployment rate is a symptom which will not disappear until all Negroes have full access to the opportunities of our society and the motivation to take advantage of them.

Unskilled workers. Unemployment rates of unskilled workers have been substantially higher than average. Here again there are many reasons, including technological progress which is reducing the demand for this type of labor, plus perhaps a somewhat looser attachment to the labor force. A return to full employment will reduce the unemployment rates here as well, but the longer-term trend is running against the unskilled. The obvious answer to their problem is to provide them with skills, but this is not so easy. First, as long as there is general unemployment, there is little need for newly trained workers. Second, the unskilled tend to be older. It is difficult to envisage how a man who has spent 30 years in unskilled physical labor can be given the types of skills for which demand is rising most rapidly.

Industries with high unemployment: Seasonal, cyclical, and declining industries. The highest unemployment rates prevail in construction, most of which is *seasonal*. In part this high rate is due to the nature of the industry; but in addition the cause must be found in the unemployment insurance system. The workers are able to receive a fraction of their normal income in the off-season. If the industry were confronted with the full social costs of seasonal unemployment, for example by an experience rating system which required employers to pay the entire cost of the unemployment benefits, there would be less seasonal unemployment. Other industries, including the apparel and the automobile industries, follow the same pattern.

When an acute labor shortage develops, as in Western Germany in recent years, even seasonal unemployment disappears. New techniques are found to build in the wintertime; other industries change their production patterns to avoid seasonal layoffs. A serious mistake may have been made in considering seasonal unemployment a purely technical matter, and our seasonal adjustment methods, which remove seasonal patterns before analysis of the figures, have deflected our attention from this important aspect of the unemployment problem.

It is inevitable that industries with high *cyclical* variation in output, primarily the producer and consumer durable sectors, will have more than average unemployment. However, in 1958–1962 cyclical unemployment has declined. The recession of 1960–1961 was the mildest of the postwar recessions, and the subsequent expansion promises to be one of the longest; there is considerable evidence that the economy is in a relatively stable state, with the inflow of orders to industry about in line with sales, with inventories in proper adjustment to production, and with fixed investment continuing at what appears to be a sustainable rate. Moreover, the federal government has finally appreciated its own role as a source of instability in the economy, and there is less hazard of the sudden swings in government orders and expenditures which contributed so importantly to earlier postwar recessions.

This decline of cyclical unemployment is one of the reasons why we must rethink our remedies. Strengthening the automatic stabilizers or giving the President standby authority for temporary tax changes will play a smaller role under these circumstances, although they still may be worthy of adoption. In any event, sooner or later the economy will again lose its present happy stability.

The problem of *industries with long-term declining employment* is concentrated in the goods-producing sector of the economy. Total goods production has increased at a very slow rate since 1955–1956. This slow increase has been combined with rapid automation and a rate of productivity advance of 3.5 per cent, substantially above the economy-wide average. Although an increase in aggregate demand would raise employment to some extent, many of these workers will never be re-employed in their old jobs. In addition, many of the semiskilled assembly line workers do not possess transferable skills. Accustomed as they have been to the relatively high wages common in organized heavy industry, they now find themselves in a very difficult position, unable to find work at their past wage rates and unable to utilize their skills.[18]

What is to be done in this situation? No doubt, some fraction of this group can be retrained. The introduction of automation can be facilitated by collective bargaining agreements which provide readjustment allowances and other benefits of a type now being pioneered in several industries. But, in the end, some highly selective reduction of the work week to spread the remaining work may be a necessary part of the solution.

Depressed areas. Even though we must be careful not to exaggerate the quantitative importance of unemployment in depressed areas, we must recognize that numbers alone do not convey the social significance of this problem. We know from studies of the Bureau of Labor Statistics [19] that unemployment in areas of substantial labor surplus differs from the national pattern: more of the unemployment is among males, more in the 25–65 age categories, more among heads of households, and more of long-term duration. In addition, some areas are more depressed than others, and the extreme cases, particularly the coal mining regions of West Virginia, Kentucky, and Pennsylvania, should stir our conscience even if they have little impact on macro-economic statistics. In these extreme cases, a combination of the worst of economic factors seems to be at work: there is no alternative economic base to the resource industries which have collapsed; workers are geographically remote so that commuting to nearby industry is impossible; for some of them the unemployment is of such long duration that the social patterns have changed in a deleterious fashion, with men doing little more than occasional jobs, but with women finding it possible to work in service and retail establishments; mobility is low, particularly for the older workers who see mining as a way of life which they refuse to abandon.

Concluding Comments

It seems that the first task in the restoration of full employment must be an increase of the general level of demand, that this increase will not develop spontaneously in the private economy unless a substantial tax reduction is enacted, and that, although a return to full employment will reduce virtually all aspects of the unemployment problem, some people in the worst of the depressed areas and some older semiskilled workers will remain in difficulty.

Furthermore, the unemployment rates for some groups in our labor force, particularly young people and Negroes, are very high even in prosperous times. General economic policies will not reduce these unemployment rates to levels that prevail for the rest of society. These high unemployment rates are symptomatic of a more fundamental failure to integrate fully members of these groups into our economic system.

Only the achievement of full employment has been considered here, and no attention has been given to other important objectives of economic policy. It seems that our society has not succeeded in reconciling true full employment with price level stability. In a world in which our trade balance is inadequate to the needs of our foreign policy and in which devaluation is an unacceptable policy instrument for the United States, the level of unemployment is in fact related to the rate of wage increase. No arguments about the favorable purchasing power effects of rising wages will change the simple fact that our economic policies over the next few years have to be as cautious as the balance of payments forces them to be. A resumption of inflation, whether due to irresponsible pricing by business or to wage increases beyond productivity gains, is the surest method of preventing a solution to the unemployment problem. Even the tougher prescription of Per Jacobssen—keeping wages stable for a period in order to bring our cost levels in line with major competitors—has much to recommend it. However, we should like some assurance that wage stability would not simply produce increased profits but would result in corresponding price reductions.

NOTES

1. President's Committee to Appraise Employment and Unemployment Statistics, "Measuring Employment and Unemployment," Washington, D.C., 1962, p. 14.

2. Edward Kalachek and Richard Westebbe, "Rates of Unemployment in Great Britain and the United States," Review of Economics and Statistics, November 1960, pp. 340–350.

3. Op. cit., Appendix A, "Comparative Levels of Unemployment in Industrial Countries," pp. 233–270, prepared for the Committee by Robert J. Myers and John H. Chandler, Bureau of Labor Statistics.

4. The Extent and Nature of Frictional Unemployment, BLS Study Paper No. 6, Study of Employment, Growth and Price Levels, Joint Economic Committee, U. S. Congress, 1959, especially pp. 1, 56, and 64.

5. Economic Report of the President, January 1962, p. 46.

6. Some parts of the study are brought up to date in the BLS paper, "Unemployment in the Early 1960's," in Unemployment: Terminology, Measurement and Analysis, Joint Economic Committee, 1961, pp. 1–96.

7. Edward Kalachek and J. W. Knowles, "Higher Unemployment Rates, 1957–1960: Structural Transformation or Inadequate Demand?" paper prepared for the Joint Economic Committee, 1961.

8. Edward F. Denison, "The Incidence of Unemployment by States and Regions, 1950 and 1960," and "The Dispersion of Unemployment among Standard Metropolitan Areas."

9. D. B. Suits, "Forecasting with an Econometric Model," American Economic Review, March 1962, pp. 116–118.

10. L. R. Klein and A. Goldberger, *An Econometric Model of the United States, 1929–1952.*

11. Gary Fromm, "Inventories, Business Cycles, and Economic Stabilization," Joint Economic Committee, 1962, p. 82.

12. J. S. Duesenberry, O. Eckstein, and G. Fromm, "A Simulation of the U. S. Economy in Recession," *Econometrica,* November 1960, pp. 789–790.

13. See Otto Eckstein, "The Tax Structure and the Functioning of the Economy," *Proceedings of the National Tax Association, 1962,* for further discussion of these points.

14. "Unemployment in America," *Newsweek,* April 1, 1963, pp. 58–71.

15. For further discussion of this point, see John T. Dunlop, "Public Policy and Unemployment," *Studies in Unemployment,* U. S. Senate Special Committee on Unemployment Problems, 1960, pp. 1–15.

16. See Seymour L. Wolfbein, "The Transition from School to Work: A Study of the School Leaver," in *Selected Readings on Unemployment,* U. S. Senate Special Committee on Unemployment Problems, p. 705.

17. For a fuller discussion, see Arthur M. and Jane N. Ross, "Employment Problems of Older Workers," *Studies in Unemployment,* U. S. Senate Special Committee on Unemployment Problems, pp. 97–120.

18. On this set of problems, see the forthcoming study by John W. Dorsey. Also see the interesting data in Bureau of Employment Security, *Family Characteristics of the Long-Term Unemployed,* a report on a study of the claimants under the Temporary Extended Unemployment Compensation Program, 1961–1962, TEUC Report No. 1, BES No. U 207-1. This study found over half of all claimants to have been laid off from manufacturing, three-fifths to be men, two-thirds heads of households.

19. Bureau of Labor Statistics, *The Structure of Unemployment in Areas of Substantial Labor Surplus,* Study Paper No. 23, Study of Employment, Growth and Price Levels, Joint Economic Committee, 1960. This study used data for the spring of 1959 and should be brought up to date.

Discussion

ALBERT REES

Dr. Heller and Dr. Eckstein devote most of their attention to the causes of our recent high levels of unemployment. Both conclude that the cause has been inadequate aggregate demand rather than structural shifts in the economy. The evidence is convincing and there is no reason to quarrel with their conclusion. In particular, it seems clear that the geographical dispersion of unemployment has been decreasing in recent years. The evidence on occupational and industrial structure is somewhat less conclusive, and work remains to be done on some dimensions of structural change, such as changes in unemployment by level of educational attainment. However, it would seem that the main concern should not be with their conclusions about the nature of our unemployment problem but with the framework within which they examine the policy alternatives confronting us. In particular, let us examine Professor Eckstein's statements that "a resumption of inflation . . . is the surest method of preventing a solution to the unemployment problem" and that "our economic policies over the next few years have to be as cautious as the balance of payments forces them to be."

It has long been commonplace in discussions of monetary and fiscal policy to argue that we must choose between the risks of high unemployment and rising prices. Events from 1958 to 1962 confirmed the existence of an inverse relationship between the level of unemployment and the rate of price increase. During this period, when the average rate of unemployment was 5½ per cent or higher in each year, the wholesale price index has not risen at all, and the rate of increase of consumer prices has slowed to about 1.2 per cent a year, a figure which is probably within the range of measurement bias. Moreover, there has been a notable lessening in the rate of increase of average hourly earnings during this period, not only in manufacturing but also in construction and trade. The annual rate of increase in average hourly earnings in manufacturing has been lower in each successive nonrecession

135

period since the Second World War, dropping from more than 10 per cent in 1947–1948 to a mere 1.5 per cent since the beginning of 1962. As a result, labor cost per unit of output in manufacturing has fallen slightly since the start of 1958. In short, we have demonstrated that inflation can be brought to a halt even in an economy with strong unions and strong oligopolies by the combined brakes of tight monetary policy and increasing marginal rates of taxation, provided that we are willing to pay the price of joblessness above the frictional level.

The central question of monetary and fiscal policy today is whether checking inflation is worth the price, for the price is very high. Avoidable unemployment of, say, 2 per cent causes a loss of real output of more than 2 per cent for a variety of reasons. The lack of demand associated with total unemployment is reflected to some extent both in shorter average hours of work for those who are employed, and in underemployment. There is an additional loss of production because output per man-hour is adversely affected by below-capacity operations. These are the factors that make up the gap between actual output and potential output which Dr. Heller has discussed.

However, this gap does not reflect the full cost of unemployment. Persistent unemployment has some costs which will be felt only in the future, and which cause reduction in potential output rather than failure to live up to the potential. For example, high levels of unemployment materially retard the flow of excess labor out of low productivity occupations, and in particular the flow of labor from agriculture into the nonagricultural sector. High unemployment intensifies the resistance of workers and unions to labor-saving innovation and leads to demands for a shorter work week. Long-term unemployment further results in a deterioration of skills and of morale of the unemployed that may impair future ability or willingness to work. In this connection it should be recalled that, when unemployment is above normal levels, long-term unemployment increases proportionately. For example, between 1957 and 1962 the number of unemployed increased 36 per cent, but the number unemployed 27 weeks or more increased 145 per cent.

We have dealt so far primarily with the economic costs of unemployment. Over and above these, there are social costs that we are only now beginning to measure. Belton Fleisher has been studying the labor market aspects of juvenile delinquency, and his preliminary results indicate a significant positive relationship between the unemployment rate of juveniles and arrests for crimes against property.

If the costs of unemployment are so high, and if we nevertheless choose high unemployment in preference to rising prices, one would imagine that the costs of rising prices are even higher. Yet there seems to be no evidence that gently rising prices have any cost at all to the economy as a whole. It is true that there have been periods in American history when full employment and rapid growth have been associated with falling prices, as in the 1880's, or with stable prices, as in the 1920's. But it is equally true that there have been periods of full employment and rapid growth accompanied by rising prices, as in the first decade of this century, or the decade following the Second World War.

There is reason to believe that gently rising prices improve the allocation of resources. Since many prices are sticky downward, the changes in relative prices required by changes in costs or in demand can take place more readily when some prices remain stable while others rise. In other words, a gently rising price level serves to lubricate adjustments in particular prices against friction.

Arguments against inflation on the ground that it causes reductions in output are at best tenuous; the true case against inflation is that it causes unintended transfers of real income. The most consistent of these transfers is, of course, that from creditors to debtors. Two important special cases of this are the transfer from the public to the government, which is always a net debtor, and the transfer away from older people who are, on the whole, net creditors. Strictly speaking, the transfers of real income from inflation arise only when the inflation is unanticipated; to the extent that it is anticipated it will be offset by rising interest rates and other changes in the terms of long-term contracts designed to preserve the intended real value of future payments. Therefore a permanent shift in monetary-fiscal policy designed to give greater weight to reducing unemployment and less weight to checking price increases would cause smaller transfers of real income after it had been in effect for some time than it would initially.* To the extent that rising prices cause unintended transfers of real income, these can be offset by deliberate policy. For example, social security payments could be raised to keep pace with the rise in consumer prices. The compensation to losers from inflation could be financed by taxing the gains of the winners. If a situation of full employment with rising prices is contrasted with a situation of unavoidable unemployment and stable prices, it is apparent that there is also another source from which to draw compensation for the losers. It can be drawn from the added production that takes place at full employment.†

It may be objected that we cannot afford to restore full employment with rising prices since this will aggravate the balance-of-payments problem. To this objection there are two answers. First, it is not certain that rising prices will in fact worsen the balance of payments; they will no doubt make the balance of trade less favorable, but they could increase private investment at home at the expense of U. S. private investment abroad by enough to offset the change in the trade balance. Second, if the balance of payments would in fact be more unfavorable at full employment, it is possible to alter our international monetary arrangements, for example by raising the selling price of gold and allowing its price to move freely between the present buying price and the higher selling price. Professional economists owe it to the public, and in particular to the unemployed and their families, to bring the issue of gold policy into the arena of open discussion.

* As Victor Fuchs has indicated, a perfectly anticipated rising price level will have less expansionary effect than an unexpected price rise, since the latter will lead to expectations of acceleration that result in attempts to spend before the pace of inflation quickens. An uneven rate of rise in prices is therefore preferable to a steady one in terms of its ability to stimulate economic activity, although it is less desirable on grounds of interpersonal equity.

† The argument is not that inflation is desirable in itself, or that raising the price level should be a deliberate aim of macro-economic policy. Rather, it suggests the following reordering of priorities: Instead of aiming at the lowest unemployment consistent with stable prices, we should aim at the smallest price increases consistent with some independently defined full-employment goal. The difference is not a trivial one.

At present it is the almost unmentionable specter haunting our policy decision and blocking the way to the creation of adequate demand. Vainly we seek to propitiate this specter by such inanities as shipping American beer to post exchanges in Munich, or we wait for it to be dissipated by rising factor prices abroad. It is fortunate for American policy makers that our unemployed have been so patient, but can we count on this indefinitely?

Suggesting that we should place more emphasis on reducing unemployment relative to other goals of policy is not to suggest that increasing aggregate demand is the only way to combat unemployment. Much can be done through retraining programs and through improvement of the labor market, and, the better the job we do along these lines, the smaller the price rise that will be associated with the return to full employment. However, it is probably an illusion to believe that our manpower and retraining policies could be so improved that we can reachieve full employment with no price rises whatever. Dr. Heller has pointed out one reason for this; wages will rise in occupations with labor shortages long before they will fall in occupations with labor surpluses, and the best that retraining programs can hope to do is to minimize this difference.

The opportunities for further training programs are illustrated by the presence, in the midst of unemployment, of labor shortages in such occupations as medical technicians and office machine repairmen. In addition to what can be done through retraining, a great deal might be accomplished by a federal program for teaching adult illiterates basic skills of reading, writing, and arithmetic. But it is generally agreed that there are grave dangers in putting exclusive reliance on the retraining and education of the unemployed without also creating more adequate demand. One danger is that many people who have been retrained at considerable cost both to the public and to themselves will still be unable to find jobs after they have completed their programs, and this will be an embittering experience. Another danger is that, without expansion of the total number of job opportunities, retrained adults will take jobs at the expense of youths just entering the labor market, and an even higher youth unemployment rate will result. Moreover, the amount of retraining that can be done under even greatly expanded public programs is small compared to the amount of private training that would be done by employers and by workers at their own expense under the stimulus of labor shortages in a larger set of occupations.

What are the implications of these remarks? First, they argue strongly for a tax reduction program of at least the size proposed by President Kennedy, but with a greater concentration of the tax reductions in the first year. They also suggest that, if tax reduction is to be imperiled or long delayed by tax reform, we should have such a reduction as soon as possible without the full program of reform, with further reduction in the higher bracket rates of the personal income tax to take place later in connection with reform and without substantial additional loss in net revenue. Finally, if we are to reduce unemployment to tolerable levels, tax reduction of the magnitudes currently under consideration cannot be relied upon to do the whole job. It should be accompanied by an expansion of the money supply and, if necessary, relaxation of the constraint that short-term interest rates cannot be allowed to fall. The latter is, of course, contingent on changes in our international monetary arrangements. High unemployment is sufficient ground for monetary ease; it should not be necessary to wait until we are already in a confirmed business contraction, when the job of restoring adequate demand will be even more difficult than it is at present.

PAUL W. McCRACKEN

There are two issues about which it ought to be possible to achieve a substantial consensus. First, in recent years a real unemployment problem has arisen. The evidence is quite clear. Our unemployment rate is higher than those for other countries, even when adjustments are made to effect definitional comparability. An increase in unemployment would be a reasonable expectation with the abnormally slow growth of recent years. And the detailed examination of unemployment data by Dr. Heller and Dr. Eckstein has developed no contrary evidence.

Second, a higher level of demand for output is essential if unemployment is to be reduced. This is not to deny that there will be a misfit between the pattern of demands for additional labor and the pattern of supplies available. The demand may appear in Iowa while the surplus supply is in West Virginia or Alaska. Or the demand may be for skilled labor while the people to be re-employed are semiskilled. Most markets in a dynamic economy are not in a state of perfect equilibrium, and the labor market is no exception.

We are entitled, however, to be reasonably sanguine about the effectiveness of market forces, if they are allowed to operate, in dealing with these disequilibria if the total demand for labor is in reasonable balance with the supply. Dr. Eckstein's data by states are instructive on this point. From 1950 to 1962 unemployment rates for only 10 of the 51 observations, including Washington, D.C., moved in a perverse direction, that is, unemployment rates above average in 1950 that moved higher in 1962, or rates that were below average in 1950 that moved still lower. The power of the market to activate equilibrating tendencies is substantial, if the total demand for labor is adequate, and this can reasonably be expected to do most of the job of fitting demands to supplies.

What problems do we confront in trying to raise the volume of aggregate demand by 5 per cent, the gap between actual and potential output discussed by Dr. Heller? There are three that deserve to be mentioned. First, there are formidable problems in getting the higher level of money demand for output. Monetary policy has been doing all that can reasonably be expected of it. The extent to which the interest rate curve can be nudged toward high short-term rates—to minimize balance-of-payments strains —and low long-term rates—to stimulate business activity—is limited, and in any case low long-term rates also create balance-of-payments problems by making our capital markets an even more attractive place for foreign long-term borrowing. Given the balance-of-payments constraint, in fact, monetary policy has been making a remarkably substantial contribution. The volume of net free reserves has been large, and the expansion of the money supply—defined, as it should be, to include time deposits—has outpaced the normal growth of the economy by a substantial margin.

In principle we could have the best of both worlds through the vigorous use of fiscal policy. This would stimulate domestic business activity, and the more active domestic demand for money would help our balance of payments. In practice we are finding that it is not so easy to make use of vigorous fiscal policy. And the problem is vastly more complex than simply that large elements of the population still hold troglodytic views about balancing the budget.

A much more fundamental problem is that we have a tax structure which has become too sensitive to changes in business conditions. Most economists have at one time or other remarked that we have built automatic stability into the economy via the tax structure. A large part of the decline in incomes during a recession is at the expense of taxes, leaving incomes after taxes more stable. The facts on this point are persuasive. The decline in federal receipts, on a national income basis, during the 1957–1958 recession was equal to 51 per cent of the decline in national income and the ratio was even higher for the 1960–1961 recession.

To an astonishing extent we have ignored the fact that the same process operates on the upswing—also acting as a powerful "stabilizer," that is, an inhibitor of expansion. From the first quarter of 1961 to the fourth quarter of 1962 the increase in federal receipts, again on a national income basis, was equal to 35 per cent of the rise in national income, and the rise in federal, state, and local receipts was equal to 45 per cent of the rise in national income. For the expansion after 1958 the ratios were very similar.

One need be no pessimist about the inherent or natural strength of the economy to suggest that this drag of the tax structure has become too severe for there to be reasonable assurance that we can operate at sustained full employment. Action in three directions is called for. First, a lowering of the tax structure would be a step forward, and it is to be hoped that the current emergent consensus in principle can bear fruit in fact.

Second, the tax structure must be made less sensitive to changes in the level of income. This means that we must work toward a slower gradient in personal tax rates, and more reliance on indirect taxes. In short, we need a less progressive tax structure, and a lesser redistribution of income via the taxing mechanism. Such a suggestion may to some seem to be turning the clock backward—or perhaps the whole calendar—but the lower income groups have more to lose through the inadequate job opportunities of an arthritic economy than through the relatively nominal redistribution of the tax load. Moreover, this incidence-of-taxation issue needs a little refocusing in its own right. We persist in looking at only half of the income-incidence of government activity, namely, the tax side. For reasons that are not at all clear we usually ignore the distribution of government services and benefits by income groups. When we include both taxes and benefits, we find that the fiscal operations of government are effecting a large redistribution of incomes toward lower income groups, and would do so even if we made our tax system somewhat less sensitive to changes in business conditions. A study of Michigan's fiscal operations in 1956, for example, showed that the net value of benefits —benefits less taxes paid—received by those with incomes less than $2,000 added about 30 per cent to their income.* The tax structure was regressive, but this fact was swamped by the enormously greater relative contribution to those with lower incomes.

Third, we must increase our capability for taking affirmative contra-cyclical action if we are to reduce the degree to which the tax structure automatically retards changes in business activity. Here the clear preference is for Presidential authority to vary tax rates over a limited range, for a designated period, and perhaps after making a full report to the Congress on reasons for his action. It is to be hoped that this item will reappear on the list of the Administration's recommendations when the tax reduction issue is resolved.

A second problem may be even more difficult. Will agglomerations of market power in labor or product markets begin to produce untenable upward pressures on costs and prices before the rise in aggregate demand achieves reasonably full employment? Perhaps not. The price level has been more stable in recent years. Wage settlements have been smaller. Foreign suppliers have added a new dimension to competitive disciplines in domestic markets. There is a degree of candor about facing this problem that did not exist a few years ago. Discussion of this problem in

* Richard A. Musgrave and D. W. Daicoff, "Who Pays the Michigan Taxes?" in *Staff Papers: Michigan Tax Study* (Lansing, 1958), p. 139.

the Economic Reports of the President for 1957 and 1958, widely criticized by economists at the time, would evoke less professional dissent now.

We may be out of the woods on this problem, but it would clearly be unwise for public policy to be based on the assumption that the wage-cost-price, market-power dimension of inflation no longer exists. The recent stability of prices may mean little more than that there is some level of underemployment that will hold the price level steady—something we have always known. Moreover, from 1959 to 1962 (both initial years after a recession) hourly earnings adjusted to exclude the effect of overtime, and inter-industry shifts increased 9 per cent. This is probably somewhat more than would be consistent with a stable cost level, even though it was a period of underemployment. Employment costs per unit of output did, in fact, rise 6 per cent during this period. Finally, a more vigorous demand for output will certainly create market conditions prompting some price increases, unless the future turns out to be a break with history.

If policies to regain full employment come to grief, there is a high probability that resumption of an untenable degree of upward wage-price pressures will be the shoals on which we run aground. If so, a research program designed to contribute to our understanding of the unemployment problem should devote substantial resources to this market-power phenomenon. If it turns out to be a problem, it is apt to be a fairly intractable one unless we get some more homework done on the matter early. This work of identifying the questions and assembling the pertinent evidence should go forward in two areas.

First, how can we reduce the market power available to unions in labor markets or to business in product markets? This might take the form of suppression of power that admittedly does exist through techniques ranging from Presidential scolding to de facto or de jure wage and price controls. Or the approach might be one of reducing the power residing in any group—a reorganization to achieve more effective market disciplines.

On this matter it is the usual custom carefully to ration exactly as many words to the monopoly power of businesses in product markets as to the power of unions to extract wage increases. In fact, it would be a remarkable coincidence if exactly half of the problem was found on each side of the boundary line. And it is at least reasonable to predict that the more difficult half of the problem will be the upward drift of labor costs per unit of output.

Second, how much inflation can we tolerate? Though a rising price level may be an unattractive prospect, we must weigh the inflation against the effects of measures necessary to eliminate it. Would willingness to accept a rising price level enable us to have more rapid economic growth? The evidence is not at all clear on this matter, and the question needs intensive and objective study. What is a reasonable expectation about the impact of inflation on decisions of consumers to buy? Available evidence suggests that it has an inhibiting effect. If we cannot have a stable price level, at least in the absence of a corset of direct controls, we had better have at hand as much objective evidence as possible on what might be expected to be the result of a rising price level.

Third, the continuing disequilibrium in our balance of payments may also turn out to be a leading contender for the honor of impeding the return to full employment. Do we have a "fundamental disequilibrium" in our balance of payments? For obvious reasons we shall continue to answer this question in the negative unless the evidence to the contrary is overwhelmingly clear. And thus we shall continue to move more cautiously on the domestic front than would be necessary if we did not need to keep one eye focused on our external payments. It is hoped that this means only a moderately delayed return to full output. In academic research, however, more resources should be devoted to the specifics of economic policy needed if it becomes ineluctably clear that we do have a "fundamental disequilibrium." If a well-thought-out plan for action failed to emerge, we would risk cowering at less than reasonably full employment until forced to extemporize when some crisis explodes.

Both Dr. Heller and Dr. Eckstein maintain that the source of the problem of unemployment is not to be found among the unemployed *per se*. It is nothing less than the problem of overall economic policy. This, it would seem, is correct. It provides a key guide line for the direction that a major part of research ought to take.

DON VIAL

It is difficult to reconcile Dr. Heller's description of the economy's ills and his analysis of its needs with the Kennedy Administration's performance to date. The analysis clearly calls for bold action; the performance is less than bold.

At the outset, it was gratifying that Dr. Heller emphasized the necessity of vastly expanding aggregate demand to achieve full employment while at the same time giving recognition to the "structural" aspects of the current unemployment problem. The AFL-CIO is in full agreement with Dr. Heller and the Council of Economic Advisers that the basic problem is one of aggregate demand, and that fiscal policies aimed at achieving a more favorable rate of economic growth must be combined with labor market programs geared to matching men and jobs and keeping the skills of our labor force abreast with technology.

Recognition of the overriding importance of the demand function does not mean that we must deny the existence of structural problems. Indeed, the structural aspects of the total problem extend beyond the retraining of those who are displaced by automation and other technological developments. They extend also to the training of those who are entering the labor market, and to the development of skills through planned, coordinated skill-development programs at the community level within the framework of an expanding economy. The point has been well made that, to the extent that we do not come to grips with structural problems, efforts to stimulate aggregate demand will be confronted with inflationary pressures earlier than they would be if men and jobs were more adequately matched through effective skill-development programs.

But the performance has not been balanced. It has been almost entirely on the structural side with the passage of the Manpower Development and Training Act, the Area Redevelopment Act, and the adjustment assistance features of the Trade Expansion Act apart from the $2.5 billion in tax relief given to business through revision of the depreciation schedules and through the investment tax credit in 1962. On the aggregate demand side, the Kennedy Administration's fiscal policies appear to combine a "hold-down" approach to public investment with tax cuts and reforms that are both inadequate and misdirected in their "mix."

In considering the stimulation of aggregate demand, very little has been said about the millions of American families in this nation of so-called affluence who live in poverty. All of the excess capacity of our economy, if put to work, would not be enough to provide these families with an American standard of living. It is obviously among the most needy that any increase in buying power would be immediately translated into effective demand. The Kennedy Administration's program seems to be lacking in this area from both a social and an economic point of view. The California Welfare Study Commission issued a report recently containing a study of "the patterns of dependent poverty in California." This study indicates that 25 per cent of California's population either lives in poverty or is on the borderline.

To single out just one example, let us consider the plight of the domestic farm worker whose wages and working conditions are an affront to the moral and social conscience of the nation. Here is an important segment of our labor force that stands at the lowest rung on the nation's economic ladder. The farm worker provides an excellent example of the failure of the classical law of supply and demand to work out in California. During the past decade a persistent shortage of domestic workers claimed by growers has actually depressed farm wages and working conditions in many crop activities. Obviously, this is a result of the *bracero* importation program.

The "trap ghetto" is another breeding ground of dependent poverty. Here, again, the Kennedy Administration's program to expand the supply of low-cost nonsegregated housing was seriously lacking.

Moving on into the area of wage and price policies, Dr. Heller has indicated that these are not "suitable vehicles for stimulating aggregate demand." The Kennedy Administration's "guideposts for noninflationary wage and price adjustments" were reasserted in the interest of "reasonable price stability" to accommodate the Administration's overriding concern with the balance-of-payments problem. Mr. Rees' comments here expose the shortcomings of the

Administration's policies in this respect. There is no economic evidence that moderate price increases are harmful to the economy. The Kennedy Administration's adherence to political "taboos" in connection with efforts to resolve the balance-of-payments problem hardly justifies the price that is being extracted in domestic policies. It appears also that Dr. Eckstein would subordinate wage policy to the balance-of-payments problem without questioning the efforts of the Administration to bring our international transactions into balance.

Beyond this, the wage policy guide lines ignore the most significant fact about wage movements in recent years. The record for 1956–1962 shows that real wages in manufacturing have failed to keep pace with productivity advancements. To argue stability in the relative shares of national income going to labor and business in the face of this experience is asking a great deal of organized labor, especially when the motivating factor behind the guideposts seems to be the balance-of-payments issue.

It is unrealistic also to ignore the substantial shift that has been taking place in the distribution of money income between families. While those in the middle ranges realized improvements in their relative shares, it is a known fact that the rich have been getting richer and the poor have been getting poorer.

The Kennedy Administration's wage policy should be concerned with more than wages in the organized sector. What about those outside of the bargaining structure? Is it the Administration's policy to accept the unhealthy trend that has taken hold in the distribution of personal income? The whole issue of wage and price policy requires a more fundamental analysis of the factors that are contributing to the imbalance between purchasing power and the nation's ability to produce.

In effecting an expansionary fiscal policy, it was pointed out that the Kennedy Administration is working on the "spending side" as well as on the "collecting side" of the federal budget. Dr. Heller made reference to a $4½ billion increase in expenditures for fiscal year 1964, but most of this, he pointed out, will be in the areas of defense and space.

California, of course, has participated handsomely in the distribution of these expenditures, but not without an awareness of the problems of imbalance created in our industrial development.

Indeed, experiences in San Diego with cut-backs and shifts in defense expenditures have shown that this is a mixed blessing. Apart from our support of U. S. policies in defense of the free world, there is little to be happy about in the fact that California manufacturing is 35 per cent defense-dependent, over 40 per cent defense-dependent in Los Angeles, and in excess of 63 per cent in San Diego. Californians would prefer greater public expenditures in the area of peaceful needs and in assistance programs to secure better balance in their industrial development.

Outside the area of defense expenditures, Californians have been advised that there will be a reshuffling of priorities in civilian programs toward those that are "most urgent." Any way you slice it, this reshuffling amounts to a "hold-down" public investment program. Such a program is particularly difficult to accept because it is known that, in our "affluent" society, many of our greatest unmet needs are in the public sector requiring huge investments by the federal government.

It was pointed out that the Kennedy Administration was contemplating a $1 billion reduction in direct loan programs—substituting loan insurance for direct lending in housing as well as in other program areas. In California, this would have a devastating effect on efforts to increase the supply of housing for the exploding population. The cut-back in direct loans for housing means an increase in mortgage interest rates and the pricing of more moderate income families out of the housing market. This cut-back in direct loans, furthermore, comes at a time when the Governor's Commission on Housing Problems has just submitted a report to the Legislature urging a vast expansion of direct loan programs to extend the housing market to low and middle income groups, to help develop balanced communities, and to prevent the further stratification of the suburbs.

It should be pointed out that the Kennedy Administration's cut-back in direct loans also has implications on the structural side of the unemployment problem. The cultural and environmental limitations of the ghetto are important factors that contribute to the school dropout problem and the underdevelopment of skills among minority groups. Rather than cut back on direct loans for housing, the Administration should move in the opposite direction. This one example emphasizes the need for the development of a federal "capital expenditures" budget to separate government investment functions from ordinary government administrative expenditures. In many other areas of urban growth the investment of government funds is vital to the stimulation of the private sector of our economy.

Turning to the Kennedy Administration's tax program, the AFL-CIO has indicated its belief that the $10 billion net tax cut proposed by President Kennedy—spread over a three-year period —will provide an insufficient stimulus to the economy. The first order of business, in labor's opinion, should be an immediate $10 billion tax cut retroactive to January 1, 1963, and concentrated in the lower income brackets to provide an immediate and necessary stimulus to consumer purchasing power. This first step tax cut would include:

1. Reduction of the present 20 per cent tax on first-bracket taxable income under $2,000 a year for a single person. This reduction would be accomplished by dividing the first bracket into two parts, with a 12 per cent tax rate applied to the first $1,000 and a 15 per cent rate applied to the second $1,000. For a married couple filing a joint return, the 12 per cent would applied to the first $2,000 of taxable income and the 15 per cent rate would be applied to the second $2,000.

2. A minimum standard deduction of $400 for an individual plus $200 for each dependent. This would be in addition to the existing personal exemption of $600 each.

3. Reduction in taxes on the first $25,000 of corporate profits from 30 per cent to 20 per cent, as proposed by the Administration. This would give quick tax relief to small businesses which are most likely to have immediate investment uses for extra money.

The AFL-CIO estimates that these three provisions, if made retroactive to the beginning of 1963, would release $10 billion into the economy—$9.8 billion in extra buying power for American families and $200 million in extra profits to small business. The "multiplier effect" would be to contribute as much as $20 billion or more to total national production, creating new jobs, providing business with investment incentives, increasing the rate of economic growth, and generating increased tax revenues.

Organized labor does not believe that the President's tax program provides the best "mix" to increase aggregate demand. Almost half of the total tax cut proposed by the Kennedy Administration—$4.8 billion—would go to corporations and to the 15 per cent of the taxpayers in the top income brackets. Furthermore, organized labor is of the opinion that President Kennedy's proposals for additional relief to stimulate investment, together with the $2.5 billion tax windfall handed business last year, are both uneconomic and unwarranted.

The so-called corporation "profit squeeze" is a myth. There is no basis for the claim that corporations lack investment money. In 1962, corporate profits after taxes reached a record high of $26 billion, and corporate dividend payments were at an all-time high of $15.9 billion—achieved while 15 per cent of productive capacity was idle. Furthermore, the availability of corporate investment money is more accurately measured internally by their "cash flow" after payment of taxes and dividends. In 1962, nonfinancial corporations amassed $35 billion in undistributed profits and depreciation set-asides. This was more money than they spent on new plant and equipment.

Clearly, the serious lag in business investment does not result from a lack of investment money, but from a lack of job-creating investment opportunities stemming from a lagging purchasing power base.

Tax reform, constituting the second phase of the AFL-CIO's tax recommendations, would be aimed at a fair distribution of the tax burden. Beyond the first-bracket tax cuts recommended by the AFL-CIO, there should be no further across-the-board reductions that are not linked to closing the loopholes that have benefited primarily the upper income groups. In this respect the 91 per cent upper tax rate is more of a fiction than a reality. An examination of the distribution of tax returns tabulated by the Internal Revenue Service indicates that there is little evidence that wealthy persons are paying 90 per cent—nor are they paying 80 per cent—nor 70 per cent—nor 60 per cent. Because of the loopholes benefiting the wealthy, the tabulations indicate that the effective top rate is in the 50 per cent range.

The loophole-closing reforms proposed by the Kennedy Administration point in the right direction, but they do not go far enough. Unfortunately, much of the revenue and equity gained from reforms would be lost as a result of the Administration's proposal to cut the capital gains tax from the present 25 per cent maximum to 19.5 per cent when it really should be raised. Furthermore, the Kennedy Administration has failed to call for the repeal of the popular "tax shelter" of the very rich—the tax-free interest income from state and local government bonds—and to ask for cuts in the excessive mineral depletion allowances.

Out of these frustrations, it is understandable that the AFL-CIO has taken such a strong position in support of a shorter work week. Many economists are less than sympathetic with this stand, not because there is no room for shortening the work week or work day on the basis of productivity increases, but because of their belief that it is not a panacea for restoring the economy to full employment. The labor movement knows that the shorter work week is not a panacea. Lacking any real evidence that the government is prepared to come to grips with the problem, however, the AFL-CIO has been left with little to turn to in the way of alternatives.

The labor movement's only reason for existence is to improve the conditions of life and labor. The federal government, by act of Congress in 1946, also has its responsibilities to pursue policies that will maintain high purchasing power and promote full employment. Thus there are mutual obligations, and the labor movement certainly cannot assume the obligations of government. In an economy of less than full employment and in the absence of effective government remedial action, the labor movement may be left with choices which are only second best.

The unemployment problem must be solved, and it must be solved soon.

PART III

WHAT CAN WE LEARN
FROM EUROPEAN EXPERIENCE?

CHAPTER 6

The Importance of Knowing What You Want

BY JACK DOWNIE

In the first postwar decade, the question "What can the United States learn from European experience?" was being asked in the reverse sense; and very naturally so, given the huge difference in income levels on the two sides of the Atlantic, the staggering expansion of production which the American economy had achieved in the preceding decade, and the presence of 70 per cent of the world's stock of monetary gold in the United States as a sort of visible symbol of the tendency for all good things to go west. Europe was living still under the shadow of the belief that, unless it could copy American methods, it would be further and further outstripped and the world would be persistently unbalanced by the Midas-touch of an ever more productive America.

With this in mind, one is tempted to answer shortly in the words of Pitt the Younger, "Roll up that map of Europe; it will not be wanted these ten years." Nor is one much dissuaded from doing so by the argument that the very success of European countries in avoiding the fate which they feared—indeed the emergence of trends the opposite of those which were thought to be likely—is evidence of the success with which the lessons of American experience were in fact learned and applied, and that this provides clear indication that, in turn, the teacher can now benefit from his former pupil. It may be that European business has learned much from America; certainly, strenuous efforts were made to persuade it to do so. But even here it is very difficult to discover specific examples where the transplantation of American ways of doing things was clearly at the root of European transformations. And it is all the more difficult in other spheres than business. But European experience perhaps at least suggests that self-questioning and the desire to question others is the first condition for improving one's performance. And, in any event, if a question is asked, it would be churlish of Europeans not to try to give the best answer that they can. But, in turn, we should bear in mind the advice of an American, Benjamin Franklin: "In this world nothing is certain but death and taxes."

It seems that people are interested in what lessons can be drawn from European experience for the better government of the United States; the question is prompted by a belief that U. S. government policy could respond more effectively to the situation of the United States. In addressing oneself to a question of this kind, one needs to bear in mind that government is a two-sided process, the action of the governing upon the governed. And hence there can be two quite different reasons why the performance of a government is responding inadequately to the demands of the situation with which it is faced. The government may be wrong or in doubt about what it ought to do. Or, knowing what it ought to do, it may be unable to do it because the governed do not accept that such action would in fact be "in the national interest." The sermon which is appropriate will vary according to the audience to which it is addressed.

It is not for a foreigner to decide whether it is the people or the government of the United States which is currently most in need of such lessons as foreign experience has to teach. And this means that he is compelled to adopt a rather less sharply directed approach than might otherwise be possible. What appears to be seemly is that he should observe what it is that people are arguing about and make such contribution as he can to the illumination of the debate. It is not true that people can be trusted always to ask themselves the questions which are most important and relevant. But one should take such self-interrogation as a starting point.

Approaching the matter in this way, Americans are found to be comparing their performance with that of European countries in respect to employment and the growth of productivity, prices, and the balance of payments. They seem to agree in concluding from these comparisons that they have something to learn about employment and growth, something to teach about price stability, and justification for a sense of grievance about the balance of payments. Thereafter there is a good deal of dispute among them about what precisely it is that they can learn from Europe about employment policy and growth.

It would appear that Europe has little to teach the United States about how to achieve strongly desired employment goals; that the United States has still something to learn about prices and incomes; and that people should not be blinded by any sense of grievance to some useful if general morals which can be drawn from balance-of-payments experience. The disagreement is not about the facts but about the interpretation to be put upon them. The statistics do no more than confirm a story which is now sufficiently well known.

Employment and Growth

One country may do more poorly than others because its task is more difficult, its capacities are more limited, or its determination to use its capacities is less.

However, the main reason for the more successful employment and growth record of European countries is not that they had an easier job. This is a particularly uncomfortable time to offer such a judgment. European growth has slackened, investment demand has weakened, and some people are beginning to suggest that we have passed a watershed and moved out of the golden light of the 1950's. The change in the labor situation and the shift in the distribution of income in Germany have stimulated some gloomy prognostications. The United Kingdom which, until now, has compensated for a rather modest growth record by a very low unemployment record, is now experiencing unemployment on a bigger scale than in any normal period since the Second World War. More generally, people are asking themselves whether it is realistic to hope that Europe can again end an investment boom without going into a slump.

Plausible theories can be built to support the view that it has been easier for Europe to grow than it has for the United States. Such theories can be summed up in a phrase of Boris Pasternak: "He was spoilt from childhood by the future, which he mastered rather early and apparently without great difficulty."

The crude notion of "catching up"—that is, the idea that countries have a certain "natural" rate of growth and that if they fall below the trend they will subsequently move back on to it at an accelerated rate—has perhaps little to commend it save such comfort to the inactive as determinism can yield. But there are more plausible versions of the thesis that the relatively rapid growth of Europe is simply a correction of past disequilibria. It may be argued that there is a natural tendency for levels of income and capital endowments per head to be roughly the same in countries where natural endowments and the quality of labor are broadly equivalent. This tendency was checked over a long period by a number of "noneconomic" factors, notably war and political confusion in Europe. But these factors have been losing their force during the 1950's, so that the disequilibrium between income and capital per head in the two areas may be expected to correct itself, with a capital flow from the United States to Europe playing a large part in the process of correction. On this view, it is only the force of external diseconomies which prevents the trickle from turning into a deluge.

And so one can go on. Reluctance to do so may be partly a burnt-child reaction to the fate of the compelling theories by which we conclusively demonstrated the inevitability of continuing continental drift in the first postwar decade. But it flows also, and more strongly, from a positive belief that the simplest explanation of the poor productivity record of the United States is its poor employment record. When simplicity goes hand in hand with plausibility, why seek the esoteric? Until such time as achieved and experienced full employment may disprove it, let us take the view that the United States does not have a growth problem, but only an employment problem. There seems to be little evidence that the problem of achieving full employment in the United States has been more difficult than that of achieving it in Europe.

This leads to an inquiry into whether there have been substantial differences in the technical capacities of governments in the two continents to influence domestic economic developments, that is, capacity to influence the level of aggregate demand and hence the level of employment and capacity working. For this purpose, governments need to know what they ought to do, to be big enough to do it, and to have instruments apt to their purpose. Again, there seems to be no clear superiority of Europe over the United States in any one of these fields.

Knowing what to do is a matter of forecasting the balance of supply and demand. This is a difficult art and it is always easy to make sport of the mistakes of its practitioners. The OECD is at present engaged in a comparison of the methods of short-period forecasting used in different countries. It is still far from complete. But the provisional conclusion is that North America has as much to teach as to learn in this field, and that, bearing in mind that much more of its forecasting has been done in the difficult conditions of underemployment, its record is no worse than most. Longer-period forecasting is an art in which no country can claim to have acquired much skill. As Bishop Butler has said, "the pretending to extraordinary revelations and gifts of the Holy Ghost is a horrid thing, a very horrid thing."

That a government should be big enough to do what is needed and should have the capacity to influence the course of aggregate demand are somewhat imprecise notions. But one may suppose that they are connected in some crude fashion with the relative importance of government transactions in total transactions. The simple indicators do not suggest any marked inferiority for the United States. Central government expenditure on goods and services, capital and current, is of roughly the same order in all the countries included, except in Germany, where the federal principle has been pushed much further than in the United States. Nor, with the same exceptions, are there great differences in the proportion of national income taken in taxes. And, although it may be argued that any administration in the United States has constitutional constraints on its freedom of maneuver to a degree unknown in Europe, experience suggests that these limitations are not decisive in practice when some course of action commands wide support.

The only major policy instrument which is found in Europe and not in the United States is the system of so-called "indicative planning," which the French have been the leaders in developing. It is, in essence, a statement, invested with the authority of the government but based on prior consultation with the interests concerned, that the pattern and level of output should move in a defined way; and that the government intends to do all in its power to ensure that these movements do in fact take place.

In France this method has certainly been associated with success throughout most of the 1950's in terms of the growth of output, and more recently by other standards also. This fact establishes some presumption in favor of attributing at least some of the success of the French economy to the efforts of the public planners. But it is very easy to fall into the trap of *post hoc ergo propter hoc*. And, although the fashion for indicative planning is now spreading, there is as yet no other major country whose experience may be used as a check on that of France. It should be remembered that, in France, the system is assisted by certain special features of the economy and by some long-standing French traditions. Because a large part of the financial machinery for collecting savings and turning them into investment capital is in the hands of the public authorities, they have powers of leverage which do not exist in most other countries. More generally, the French system may be seen as squarely in the main stream of a tradition of cooperation between government and industry which goes back at least to the time of Colbert.

In any event, whatever be the virtues of planning in the French sense—or in the Swedish, Dutch, or British senses for that matter —it is not conceived of by its authors as primarily an instrument of employment policy. And it is with the unsatisfactory employment record in the United States that we are here concerned.

Having concluded that European countries had no pre-eminent advantages in respect to the task they faced or the capacities at their disposal, we are led to conclude, by exclusion, that the major reason why most of them have done better than the United States is that Europeans have been more determined that governmental capacities should be used. On this view, what European experience has to teach people in the United States is that people tend to get whatever it is that they want most.

It is not necessary, perhaps, to spend time laboring the contrast between the political cash value which full employment has had in most European countries and the political tolerance for unemployment which has existed, and still exists, in the United States. The contrast is so striking that it was natural to give credence to the view, now abandoned, that American methods of measuring unemployment exaggerated it greatly and that there was not "really" so much difference between the United States and Europe. But one is unavoidably driven to ask what other policy objectives have been set above that of employment.

The answer seems to be, in considerable measure, the negative objective of avoiding strong and purposeful government of economic affairs. Nor is it, perhaps, surprising that this should have been so. The strength and antiquity of the American belief in the desirability of market solutions—typified by the requirement in the Employment Act of 1946 that the government should act to maintain employment ". . . in a manner calculated to foster and promote free competitive enterprise . . ."—is something of which a European needs constantly to remind himself. He needs to remind himself also that one of the fundamental reasons why there is such a difference from the European belief that government is a difficult but necessary and highly valuable art is the immutable fact of the continental dimensions of the United States. The problem of reconciling the conflicts of different interest groups, which is what government is about, comes near to being different in kind when the population in question is raised by a factor of four and the area by one of fifteen.

Traditional attitudes were doubtless strengthened for a time by the accidents of postwar experience. The remarkable responsiveness of the American economy to the excesses of demand to which it was subjected in the earlier postwar years was a powerful reinforcement for the hope that, having been equipped with some improved built-in stabilizers, the American economy could be relied on always to find an even keel by itself, and that a hands-off policy by the government might positively help it to do so. It is perhaps not surprising that a certain number of lean years

had to be experienced before this belief began to be shaken.
But the United States has experienced several lean years, and
we are still witnessing the remarkable spectacle of an administration laboring to convince its public that unemployment matters
and to convince their elected representatives that a reduction in
the tax burden may be nationally as well as privately rewarding.
It is hard to believe that the negative objective of avoiding government can be so powerful as to provide the whole explanation.

It is always unwise to shun the obvious. And the most obvious
explanation, which fits not only the facts but also what people
have said, is quite simply that Americans weakly chose employment because they chose price stability strongly. It may be that
"price stability" has often been used as a convenient shorthand
for "sound economic policies," in which were included the negative objectives discussed above. But it is hard to avoid the conclusion that the contrast between European and American price
history from 1956 to 1962 is an accurate index of a contrast in
attitudes. Much has been said in Europe about the importance of
price stability. But nowhere—not even in Germany, supposedly
the classic example of inflation neurosis—have countries been prepared in the event to arrest their growth and create unemployment simply in order to stop prices from rising.

Prices and Incomes

One cannot criticize a choice of price stability over employment. But it is important to emphasize that the simplest and most
convincing *ex post* explanation of the poor growth and employment record is that, explicitly or implicitly, such a choice was
made in the United States. For, otherwise, there is a danger that
people will come to believe that an acceptable solution for the
price problem has been found. Much of the comment on the end
of the age of inflation which one reads today leads one to fear
that precisely this error is being made.

In 1956, in a paper contributed to a National Planning Association 10th Anniversary Symposium on the Employment Act, Mr.
James Tobin wrote: *

---

* *In The Employment Act Past and Future* (ed. Gerhard Colm), National
Planning Association, 1956, "The Interdependence between an Effective
Stabilization Policy and the Attitudes of Labor," by James Tobin, p. 114.

. . . The nightmare of an economy of special interest groups who use their economic and political power to escalate wages and prices upwards in a continuous competitive scramble has given way to the American dream of an evergrowing full employment economy with a stable, or at worst slowly rising, price level. Economists are notoriously susceptible to the current economic climate, and we should not be guilty today of dismissing too hastily the problems that seemed so formidable only five years ago.

Since then, American opinion has gone through another full cycle; a return of the nightmare which, *inter alia,* gave birth to the massive study of the Joint Economic Committee; and its subsequent re-evaporation under the benevolent light of the price and cost experience of 1958–1962.

Even economists learn, and this is not to suggest that many people in the United States do not now recognize that price stability is something which can be maintained, if at all, only by strenuous and constant effort. But it seems that there is, nevertheless, a danger that the problem will be neglected until it forces attention, in the shape of an embarrassing choice, when the level of employment begins to rise again. This danger is all the stronger because the nature of the problem is frequently misconstrued.

The 1962 Report of the Council of Economic Advisers, in its discussion of prices, notes that "at least in the short run, there is considerable room for the exercise of private power, and a parallel need for the assumption of private responsibility." The implication is that it is essentially the existence of imperfections in the competitive system which creates a problem of prices, and that when there are no imperfections the natural workings of the competitive system will ensure zero cost and price changes. This view seems to be characteristic of much American thinking.

The theoretical formulation of reasons for believing this view to be wrong is that the demand and supply curves for the (closed) economy as a whole are not independent of each other, but identically equal, so that the notion of an equilibrium price, which has meaning in particular equilibrium analysis, has no meaning here. Translated into common sense terms, this means that, if any particular set of employers know that the rate of wage increase they grant will be generalized throughout the economy, they will not be restrained from granting it by the knowledge that it will be necessary to raise prices to compensate for it.

If the supply of money is taken as independently given, then, even in a closed economy, the price level ceases to be completely indeterminate. This corresponds to the common sense notion that at some level of unemployment the price level will be stable and that, if the money supply is kept constant, a general price rise will eventually be brought to an end through the medium of the unemployment which the increasing tightness of money produces. And one may go on, introducing further constraints into the model and approaching closer to determinacy.

This point of the absence of theoretical justification for considering price stability as the normal product of a competitive economy has been emphasized because it has important practical consequences. If one believes that it is only the imperfections of competition which make it difficult to maintain stable prices in conditions of full employment and rising output, one will be led to seek atavistic kinds of solutions for the problem. Attention will be directed toward securing a return to the primitive virtues. Consider, for example, this extract from the memorandum of reservation entered by Professors Fellner and Lutz in the OEEC report on *The Problem of Rising Prices.**

. . . The future is unpredictable and it might turn out that, given the present bargaining systems and the prevalent attitudes of the bargaining parties, the prevention of wage-push inflation would, even in the years ahead, require unreasonably low levels of employment . . . in this event we would urge making it clear to the public that wage bargaining between powerful groups has become incompatible with a reasonable employment policy . . . collective bargaining for wages by large unions would not be needed to protect labor's interests. . . . On neither side of the labor market should the permissible size and the permissible functions of organizational units be regarded as immutable.

If, on the other hand, one believes that a fully employed economy has no natural tendency toward price stability, one will be driven instead to seek radical solutions, in the shape of new methods of income and price determination. A steadily growing conviction in Europe of the need for such radical solutions—the need for what has come to be called an incomes policy—is, it appears, one of the most important lessons Europe offers to the United States.

* Published by OEEC in May 1961.

This is not to say that European experience yet provides a recipe book on how to run an incomes policy. Most European countries are still at the beginning of their search for an effective policy. And, in any case, the mechanisms by which incomes get settled, the institutions and the traditions, vary so much from country to country that it will rarely be possible to transfer the detail of one country's experience to another country. Nevertheless, European experience already has something to teach the United States about the nature of the problem and the sort of conditions which a solution must satisfy.

The problem is how to handle the very fundamental interest conflicts which arise over the distribution of the national income. Traditionally, this has been left to be settled in a decentralized fashion through the workings of the market. The government has stepped in only as midwife, when the birth of new agreements was proving unduly prolonged and painful, or, after the event, to remedy by use of its fiscal powers any really dangerous anomalies to which the competitive processes had given rise. Definition of the national interest by the government, which is the sign that an interest conflict is being transferred to the center, has not been customary with respect to such primary settlements. This studied failure to intervene in such settlements has been in conformity with the normal democratic rule that one does not bring conflicts to the center for settlement if one can avoid doing so. Given the strength of this presumption, it is scarcely surprising that governments have moved toward accepting the need to define the national interest in income settlements with marked reluctance. But many European governments nevertheless have come to feel that events compel them to make this move.

When the ice has thus been broken, governments have immediately been confronted with the problem of how to make *effective* statements; how to define the national interest in a way which is relevant to the processes of decision making which are involved in income determination.

The first lesson they have learned is that they are likely to fail if they confine themselves to certain classes of income; the present transition in terminology from wages policy to incomes policy is much more than a change in words. The immediate and natural reaction of wage earners to the suggestion that considerations of the national interest should enter into wage determination was the claim that what was good for them was good for other classes of income also. The need to accommodate this reaction makes it harder to work out a policy. But it is an important step forward when governments recognize the need as a fact of life.

The next discovery has been how difficult it is to frame general statements of what the national interest requires in terms which allow one to verify after the event whether any particular income or price decision has conformed to the advice. And this, after all, is the minimum requirement for an effective policy. An American example—the guideposts, suggested in the 1962 Report of the Council of Economic Advisers—may serve as an illustration. The guidance offered to price setters is the relation between their industry's rate of productivity increase and that of the economy as a whole. Wherever it is appropriate to think of the industry as setting prices, this guidepost can clearly be effective; the Kennedy Administration found it possible to say unequivocally in 1962 that, in raising its prices, the steel industry was behaving contrary to the national interest. But it is typically the individual company which determines price policy, and in such cases there appears a sharp conflict between the guidance and some of the essential practices of a market economy. If a company is particularly efficient (low cost), it is neither normal nor desirable that it should immediately reduce its prices below the point necessary to attract demand for the whole of its output; the "excess profits" which it then earns provide the means for the expansion which will justify a further reduction in prices subsequently. There is in fact a dilemma: how to make statements which mean something without being driven into a multitude of definitions of the national interest corresponding to the multitude of income and price determinations which occur. The dilemma is most acute in pricing, because of the greater decentralization of decision making. But it is in fact quite general.

As and when some means is found of making statements of the national interest which are verifiable in principle, governments are confronted with the need for information to translate principle into practice. An increasing number of European countries have been finding that they simply do not have the information which is needed to carry out an incomes policy. The minimum requirement is information on the level and rates of growth of the classes of income which are significant for the processes of income determination particular to the economy in question. In most countries, however, such data on incomes as exist have usually been collected with other purposes in mind, and rarely meet the present need. It is doubtful that the United States will find itself much better provided. Since it usually takes a long time to organize new statistical sources, it is never too soon to start.

Finally, and perhaps most important of all, how severe should be the standards which countries set themselves in this matter of price stability? This is ultimately a matter of values. In any event, European experience is still too scanty to offer much guidance on the conditions for varying degrees of success. But it seems that the sort of price record which the United States has had in the 1958–1962 period is more than it is reasonable to hope for in a fully employed, rapidly growing economy. The experience of Europe, and particularly the remarkable restoration of faith in money which we have witnessed in France and Germany, gives some warrant for hoping that such strict canons of monetary behavior are unnecessary as well as unattainable.

The Balance of Payments

It was suggested earlier that Americans thought they had something to learn about employment and growth and something to teach about prices, but that on the balance of payments they mostly felt aggrieved. If employment and growth objectives are now being accorded a higher priority in the American scale, it is inevitably frustrating to find that the government's ability to move more strongly in pursuit of these objectives is constrained by the deficit in the balance of payments. Frustration is turned to irritation by the belief that the balance-of-payments deficit results in considerable measure from the inappropriate distribution of military and development lending responsibilities between the United States and European countries.

This view collides with the alternative view of many Europeans that the trouble lies rather in the scale on which the private sector in the United States is acquiring capital assets in other countries. At the next remove, there is a further argument about whether the blame for such international problems as may be created by movements on long-term capital account is to be laid at the door of American or European policies. These are not statistical or analytical questions; an infinite variety of partial balances can be shown to be equal to the United States balance-of-payments deficit, but no one of them is therefore the "cause" of the deficit; the arguments are rather about political values and standards.

European experience is in principle relevant to the more mundane question of how the United States could—as opposed to should—solve its external problem. And the persistence of large external surpluses in continental Europe from 1952 to 1962 might suggest that Europe had much to teach in practice. But, in fact, the scope for advising America from the experience of Europe is limited because, in large measure, Europe's strength on external account and the United States' weakness have been two sides of the same coin. With the outcome jointly determined in this way, it is very difficult to say that this or that aspect of European policies was instrumental in creating a strong balance-of-payments position. With the United States deficit so large and long-standing, there have been very few examples of major European countries' achieving balance of payments transformations from sustained deficit to balance or surplus. The United Kingdom, where such a transformation has been perhaps most necessary, and whose situation in many ways closely resembles that of the United States, has not in fact done better than keep its nose above the water. France is a striking example of a country which, having lived externally in queer street throughout most of the postwar period, achieved a remarkable transformation in 1959 and has since maintained the strength then acquired. But there were many special elements in the French transformation—in particular the readiness of other countries to accept a change in the relative exchange value of the franc and a special concatenation of domestic political circumstances which made it possible to avoid the devaluation's being offset by internal cost increases.

There are, however, a limited number of morals from European experience which are relevant to the United States. The first relates to self-help. It is now universally recognized in Europe, not only in theory but also in practice, that there are two sides to a balance of payments, a deficit in one place implying a surplus in another. In recent years there has been a good deal of discussion of the responsibilities of surplus countries for contributing to the correction of international disequilibrium. And there have been some substantial practical contributions to match this growing understanding. But the brute fact still remains that a country which is gaining reserves can, in principle, go on doing so indefinitely whereas the country which is losing them can do so only for a finite period. And this difference in the imperatives of reality is matched by a continuing difference in attitudes. However much it may be recognized that surplus countries have their responsibilities, a deficit country is still regarded as carrying the primary responsibility for curing its deficit. The question "How can I cure my deficit?" is one which the deficit country must, in the last resort, address to and answer itself.

The second moral was drawn nearly 20 years ago. In his last article, published posthumously in the Economic Journal, J. M. Keynes * said:

. . . The pressure on the rest of the world from 1930 onwards was due to a large-scale capital movement from Europe to America being superimposed on a substantial, but not unwieldy, balance on current account. The serious consequences to the rest of the world flowed from the anomaly of a country with a substantial favourable balance being simultaneously the recipient of investible funds from abroad.

If the terms United States and Europe are interchanged in this passage, we have not a bad description of the balance-of-payments situation of today. The fact is that the countries which have a strong current account position have more often than not had strong positions on capital account also; both France and Germany have provided striking examples of this association. Perhaps, indeed, it is time that we ceased to regard such associations as anomalies. Strong current account positions have tended to be associated with strongly competitive cost positions and rapid rates of growth, thus offering attractive prospects of capital gain to the investor. And, the stronger a country's position on overall external account has been, the more likely has the speculator thought it that there was a capital gain to be secured through

* John M. Keynes, "The Balance of Payments of the United States," Economic Journal, Volume LVI, No. 222, June 1946, p. 173.

exchange rate appreciation. The frequent disappointment of such speculative hopes has not destroyed their allure. While this point may be considered cold comfort at the moment, it suggests that, when the U. S. balance of payments begins to right itself decisively, it will move much faster than we think.

The fundamental condition for such a decisive change is that costs in the United States should be in appropriate relationship to those in Europe. While recent European experience has shown mainly that it is impossible to hold an unduly low level of costs against the pressures of the external surplus which it generates, United States' experience in the future may be expected to demonstrate that the improvement in costs which has occurred will generate the needed improvement on current account. From this standpoint, the earlier choice of price stability before employment will pay dividends; the problem will be, as discussed earlier, to hold costs when unemployment recedes.

But an interim has to be lived through which may require independent action on capital account. This fact leads to a final point which will be posed as a question rather than offered as an answer. In Europe it is thought to be both right and unavoidable to allow policies affecting the money and capital markets to be very heavily conditioned by external circumstances. The United Kingdom, for example, has shown repeatedly that tight and dear money can bring about quickly, and maintain, big improvements on capital account. The German monetary authorities, having an external surplus, have been pursuing an easy or neutral policy for the last 2½ years, in spite of the fact that, for most of the time, they were confronted with a roaring boom. In the United States, by contrast, the authorities—both monetary and debt management—have apparently been forced to engage in a continuous effort of defensive explanation for concessions to external considerations which many people in Europe have thought unduly modest.

This contrast in attitudes and in practice is clearly yet another reflection of the difference in size between the United States and any single European country. There are few European money and capital markets which cannot be swamped by international movements, as indeed the German market was in 1961 when the authorities at first sought to counter the boom with an active monetary policy. By contrast, the United States market is dominated by domestic flows; the flow of foreign money can never be large in relation to these, and even international movements of American money, while they may be large in balance-of-payments terms, are likely to be only marginal by the standards of the capital market.

The psychological implications of this difference are easy to see; in the United States, it is much more difficult to get acceptance for externally oriented monetary and debt management policies. What is less clear is whether, from a technical standpoint, the proportionately limited magnitude of the external factor leaves the United States authorities without the strength to maintain the unusual relation between monetary conditions and the state of the economy which is called for when external and internal considerations are pointing in opposite directions.

This last circumstance is sufficiently common these days for the answer to this question to be of the first importance.

> "Now you have seen what we can do. Now want it!
> and if you do, we will achieve an art." WAGNER

CHAPTER 7

Unemployment in Western Europe and the United States

BY ROBERT J. MYERS

The recent unemployment experience of five leading industrial countries of Western Europe with a combined population of over 200 million and a combined labor force of some 93 million—about a third larger than our own—indicated in 1962 a total of only about 2.1 million unemployed as compared with 4.0 million in this country. From 1958 to 1962, when joblessness in these countries was hovering around 1, 2, or 3 per cent, our own rate never fell below 5 per cent and averaged 6 per cent.

The difference between our unemployment rate and the average for these European countries was only a little more than 3 percentage points. But, if we could wipe out that difference, it would mean 2 million more jobs, and perhaps $40 to $50 billion in Gross National Product. We can surely be excused for looking enviously at our European friends to see how they do it. We have profited much in the past from exchange of ideas with Europe. It

172

would be short-sighted indeed to ignore Europe's recent success in holding down unemployment.

Comparative Levels of Unemployment

Before considering the factors that account for Europe's happier experience with unemployment, however, let us deal briefly with the often expressed suspicion that the difference between jobless rates here and across the sea is largely an illusion, arising out of differences in definitions and statistical methods used in counting the unemployed. It has even been suggested that, if we would only adopt the more restrictive definitions used in Europe, we would already be a long step forward in solving our unemployment problem.

During 1961 and 1962 the Bureau of Labor Statistics looked into the question of comparability in some detail. Its efforts were accelerated after President Kennedy expressed interest in the matter late in 1961, in appointing the President's Committee to Appraise Employment and Unemployment Statistics—the "Gordon Committee." The findings of that committee need to be summarized here only briefly.[1]

The most widely published and most commonly quoted statistics on unemployment in European countries are indeed quite different from our own and are usually based on registrations at placement offices or the records of unemployment insurance or public relief agencies. Fortunately, most of these countries have also had a try at the sample survey approach to unemployment measurement, sometimes referred to as the "American system." The official monthly unemployment statistics in Japan and Canada are now very similar to our own. The Federal Republic of Germany, Italy, and Sweden have periodic sample surveys in addition to other, more widely known, systems of measurement. France has made sample surveys irregularly and somewhat experimentally since 1950. Only Great Britain has never made a labor force sample survey, but with respect to that country we have had the advantage of intensive research by a competent labor economist over a period of nearly a year.[2]

The sample surveys have not always used the same concepts and definitions as our own, but their general pattern has been the same as ours and the definitions, where they have differed,

TABLE 1. Number of Unemployed and Rates of Unemployment, as Published and Adjusted to U. S. Definitions, Eight Industrial Countries, 1960–1962

| | As Published [a] | | | | | | Adjusted to U. S. Definitions | | | | |
| | Number Unemployed (thousands) | | | Rate | | | 1960 Estimates | | | Preliminary Rates | |
Country	1960	1961	1962	1960	1961	1962 [b]	Labor Force (millions)	Number of Unemployed (thousands)	Rate	1961 [b]	1962 [b]
United States	3,931	4,806	4,007	5.6	6.7	5.6	70.6	3,931	5.6	6.7	5.6
Canada	448	469	391	7.0	7.2	6.0	6.4	448	7.0	7.2	6.0
France	131	112	122	1.0 [c]	0.9	0.9	19.1	370	1.9	1.7	1.8
Germany (FR)	237	161	142	1.2	0.8	0.7	25.2	245	1.0	0.5	[d]
Great Britain	360	341	463	1.6	1.4	1.9	23.9	570	2.4	2.2	2.8
Italy	1,746 [c]	1,608	1,333	8.2 [c]	7.6	6.3	20.9	896	4.3	3.7	3.2
Japan	430	390	418	1.0	0.9	0.9	43.5	480	1.1	1.0	1.0
Sweden	19	17	19	1.4	1.2	1.3	3.7	56	[d]	1.5	1.5

[a] From ILO *Year Book of Labor Statistics* and *International Labour Review,* and from national publications.
[b] Preliminary figures in some cases based on reports for less than full year.
[c] Revised figure.
[d] Not available.

have been reasonably explicit. The surveys have been conducted by competent statisticians. Much supplementary information, facilitating adjustment for differences in definitions, has been obtained. It has thus been possible to arrive at an estimate of the number of unemployed in each country measured in accordance with United States definitions and methods.

Unemployment rates for each country for the years 1960–1962 —as published and after adjustment to United States definitions— are presented in Table 1. It is noteworthy that adjustment to United States definitions does not change the comparative position of the United States very much. The adjustments result in lowering the unemployment rate of the foreign countries more frequently than raising them. The adjusted figures for 1962 show this country second only to Canada in rate of unemployment, instead of third, after Canada and Italy, in terms of the unadjusted figures.[3] The average rate of unemployment among the five European countries was a little lower after adjustment to United States definitions.

The foregoing comparisons relate, of course, exclusively to "western" nations. In the communist countries, where freedom from unemployment is generally accepted as dogma, it is not to be expected that similar figures will exist.

In this respect as in many others, however, Yugoslavia is an exception. That country regularly publishes the number of unemployed, from which can be computed unemployment rates not dissimilar from our own. The figures for 1960, 1961, and 1962 are:

Year	Number (thousands)	Rate
1960	159	5.2 [4]
1961	191	5.7
1962 (9 mos.)	235	6.9

The U.S.S.R. is still riding the crest of a vigorous postwar economic expansion. The state has unquestioned authority to assign workers to jobs and to direct plant superintendents to hire them. There is widespread evidence of labor shortage in skilled jobs and, in Siberia, in other jobs as well. Under these circumstances it might be expected that unemployment in that country would actually approach the zero level that is claimed.

The Bureau of Labor Statistics is carrying on continuing research on the subject of manpower in the U.S.S.R.[5] Few solid conclusions have yet been formulated, but it is clear that that country has not been able to guarantee its citizens freedom from joblessness. On the one hand, the reversion from Stalinism has led to a partial abandonment of the policy of forced labor and reliance to a considerable extent on "inducements" and persuasion, which are not always effective in attracting workers or in holding them.[6] Labor turnover is thus a serious problem.[7] Incredible though it may seem, moreover, there is no coordinated system of placement agencies in the U.S.S.R. The job offered to a worker may be so unattractive in terms of duties, pay, housing, or transportation that the worker is unwilling to accept it. The time required to get into a new job may thus run to several weeks.[8]

Despite the strong authority of the state, therefore, the job-creating influence of a rapidly growing economy, and the unquestionable evidence of labor shortages in some areas, measurable unemployment undoubtedly exists in the U.S.S.R. One might conclude tentatively that it would amount to appreciably more than in the faster growing capitalist economies, such as Japan and Germany, although very substantially less than in this country.

Causal Factors

Since unemployment is indeed much lower among the industrial countries of Europe than in the United States, we will not be wasting our time if we ask how that comes about.

Growth of the labor force. To begin with, it is desirable to look at the characteristics of our labor force. Is it possible that peculiar disadvantages in rate of growth or in sex or age distribution make high unemployment almost inevitable? Our labor force has grown rapidly, calling for the creation of about 8 million new jobs between 1951 and 1960 if unemployment was to be held constant. The 12 per cent increase in our labor force in this period, however, compared with a similar figure in Sweden, 18 per cent in Germany, 23 per cent in Canada, and 25 per cent in Japan. Labor force growth was less in France, Great Britain, and Italy; perhaps this fact makes high employment more easily attainable. But there is little evidence that labor force growth is an insuperable obstacle to reasonably full employment in the United States.

Women workers. Our high proportion of women workers, now about one-third of the labor force, is another possible factor, for unemployment rates are almost invariably higher among women than among men. France, Great Britain, and Sweden have about the same proportion of women workers as we have, however; and women make up about 37 per cent of the labor force in Germany and about 40 per cent in Japan.

Young workers. The unemployment rate for persons under 20 is nearly three times as high as for adults, and this group made up about 8 per cent of our labor force in 1960. But young people were equally important in the labor force of France. And in the other western countries they were relatively *more* numerous—13 per cent in Germany, for example. Not one of these countries had a higher proportion of its workers in the favorable age group 20–64 than we had.

Consideration of these demographic factors, therefore, yields little comfort and little help. There are a number of economic factors, however, that are somewhat more helpful in explaining our relatively high rates of unemployment.

Decline of agriculture. One of these factors is the relatively minor importance of agriculture as a source of employment. Unemployment is much less frequently associated with agriculture than with industry, partly because agriculture is less susceptible to cyclical change, but chiefly because a high proportion of the workers in farming are self-employed or unpaid family workers, who tend, in slack periods, to work part-time or withdraw from the labor force rather than seek another job with pay.

Agriculture has been declining relatively as a source of employment in all the countries studied, and in our own country the decline has been absolute as well as relative. We must look back as far as the 1830's to find a period when as few of our workers were in agriculture as today. In 1960 about one worker out of twelve in our labor force was in agriculture, as compared with about one out of three in Italy and Japan, and one out of four in France. Only Great Britain, with one in twenty, has relatively fewer workers in agriculture.

High proportion of wage and salary workers. Relatively more of our workers work for a wage or salary and are thus particularly susceptible to unemployment. This factor is, of course, closely related to the point just discussed, since only a few of those in the agricultural labor force work for a wage or salary. Wage and salary workers in 1960 accounted for fully 84 per cent of our labor force, but only 77 per cent in Germany and Sweden, 66 per cent in France, and 62 per cent in Italy. Only Great Britain, with 90 per cent, had relatively more of its labor force working for a wage or salary.

If unpaid family workers made up about 30 per cent of our labor force and employers and the self-employed another 24 per cent, as in Japan, the change in weights alone, without any change in the unemployment rates for the various worker groups, would have reduced our overall rate to 3.7 per cent.

Structural unemployment. Such factors as displacement of workers as a result of changes in demand, decline of occupations due to technological advance, and the changing economic condition of specific localities are important potential causes of unemployment in this country. It would be erroneous to conclude, however, that structural change is less prevalent or less far-reaching in Europe than it is here. To illustrate the powerful changes that have made themselves felt in Europe, it is only necessary to mention the decline of the coal mining areas of the Loire and Cevennes in France, the immigration of hordes of escapees from communism into the Federal Republic of Germany, the virtual disintegration, at one time, of the economy of southern Italy, and the impact of the Common Market on production patterns in all of Western Europe.

There is no adequate measure of the extent of structural change in the various countries, but it is instructive to look at the data on relative changes in productivity. Although certainly inadequate, they may reflect structural change more reliably than any other available measures. Between 1951 and 1960 real GNP per capita in the United States, up 12 per cent, rose less than in any of the other seven industrial countries except Canada. The increase for Italy was 58 per cent, for Germany (F.R.) 70 per cent, and for Japan 90 per cent. Manufacturing production per person employed in manufacturing rose less in this country than in any of the others.

Lagging economic growth. As a final and very important difference that may help to explain the different unemployment rates in the United States and the industrial countries of Western Europe, one must consider differences in their rates of economic growth. Economic growth, together with changes in productivity, largely determines the demand for labor. The expansion of the economy must be sufficient to offset gains in productivity and to absorb the growth of the labor force if unemployment is to be held at a given level.

Table 2 shows the average annual percentage increase in real

TABLE 2. RATE OF ECONOMIC GROWTH, 1951–1960 [a]

| Country | Average Annual Increase (in per cent) | |
	Real Gross National Product	Industrial Production
United States	2.9	3.2
Canada	3.6	4.3
France	4.2	6.6
Germany (F.R.)	7.2	8.8
Great Britain	2.7	3.2
Italy	5.8	8.5
Japan	8.7	14.5
Sweden	3.7	3.7

[a] Sources: OEEC, Gencral Statistics, March 1961 and July 1961; Chase Manhattan Bank, New York, The New European Market; A Guide for American Businessmen, April 1961; and national sources. Rates for Canada and Japan were computed by author.

GNP and in industrial production in eight industrial countries from 1951 to 1960, inclusive. It is apparent that all the countries except Great Britain experienced a more rapid growth than did the United States.[9] The countries with the most rapid growth, Germany (F.R.) and Japan, were those that have recently shown

the lowest levels of unemployment. The growth experienced in
the other countries as a whole was about three-quarters greater
than that for the United States. When it is considered that even
the relatively modest economic growth experienced by the United
States resulted in an employment increase of about 6 million, or
9 per cent, from 1951 to 1960, it is immediately apparent how
quickly the number of unemployed (which averaged 3.9 million
in 1960 and 4.0 million in 1962) would dwindle with a growth
rate as high as the average for the other countries.

Social Attitudes and Administrative Programs

The lessons we can learn from the foregoing remarks have unfortunately little practical usefulness for us. For the most part,
we can never hope to apply them. They suggest that, *if* a larger
proportion of our labor force were in agriculture, *if* we had relatively fewer wage and salary workers, *if* we had fewer young
people in the labor force, and *if* we could anticipate less structural
change in the future, then, other things being equal, we could
expect to achieve a lower level of unemployment. But these
changes are not in the cards.

The one area in which we have a good chance of reducing our
vulnerability to unemployment is that of economic growth. We
shall return to this topic briefly below. But first let us consider a
number of other respects in which our economy contrasts with
those of Europe—matters relating primarily to laws, social attitudes, and administrative programs and clearly within our power
to change.

Job security. One of the differences lies in our attitude toward
layoffs. The typical American employer is not indifferent to the
welfare of his work force, but his relationship to his workers is
often rather impersonal. The interests of his own employers, the
stockholders, tend to make him extremely sensitive to profits and
to costs. When business falls off, he soon begins to think of reduction in force, which he hopes will be temporary. If it runs on for
an extended period, however, there is little he can do about it
until business picks up. His discomfort over the layoffs may be
relieved somewhat by reflecting that his workers will receive unemployment benefits, perhaps augmented by Supplementary Unemployment Benefits, for which he helps to pay.

In many other industrial countries, specific laws, collective agreements, or vigorous public opinion protect the workers against layoffs except under the most critical circumstances. Despite falling demand, the employer counts on retraining his permanent employees. He is obligated to find work for them to do.

In Italy the position of the worker who is part of the regular work force is effectively protected by laws and collective agreements. Although not impossible, it is both difficult and costly for an employer to accomplish a reduction in force. Regular workers have a high degree of job security. In Belgium under the law of February 14, 1961, the king is empowered under certain conditions to make layoffs, dismissals, or short-time subject to prior authorization or declaration.

In the United Kingdom, France, Germany, and certain other countries, the law goes less far in assuring job security than in Italy, but social pressure makes employers feel a strong sense of responsibility for permanent workers. This social attitude was behind the feeling of indignation and outrage recently expressed in France when the branch factories of certain American employers abruptly announced layoffs of many French employees when business began to decline.

There is probably no country in the world where the worker who has attained permanent status has greater job security than in Japan. Many such workers enter their jobs directly from school and stay there until retirement.

These arrangements are certainly effective in holding down unemployment. But they involve a very heavy cost. They partly explain the traditionally lower productivity and lower income levels in other countries. Here is something we can learn from our neighbors, therefore, but are we quite sure we want to learn it? Are there not better ways to reduce unemployment?

Unemployment insurance. We need deal but briefly with unemployment insurance, separation payments, and similar benefits, which are palliatives rather than remedies. We began to learn this part of our lesson later than some other countries, but we have learned it pretty well. The vast majority of our workers are now protected by such insurance, including both obligatory and voluntary systems. The liberality of unemployment insurance is extremely difficult to judge. Beyond question, many workers in this country receive a higher income during periods of unemployment than fully employed workers are paid in some other countries. Broad unemployment insurance is an indispensable requirement in a high-productivity economy in which employment fluctuates with business conditions.

Training and retraining. We have much to learn with respect to training and retraining for jobs. This is particularly important in relation to new workers preparing to enter the labor market and to experienced workers whose jobs have disappeared as a result of technological change. The training programs of such countries as Sweden, the United Kingdom, and France play an important part in preparing workers for jobs. Not only training in public facilities is involved, but also a great deal of training in private industry, which differs from our own training in industry in that it is often part of a public program and may be subsidized through payments to employers.

Higher unemployment among American youths seems to be an important factor in accounting for our higher overall unemployment rate than that in Great Britain. Joseph Zeisel has found that the comprehensive national vocational guidance system, formal apprenticeships, and other training programs for youth in Great Britain help explain the difference.[10] In a recent year about 35 per cent of the boys and about 10 per cent of the girls getting out of school in that country were apprenticed to skilled crafts or undergoing training for recognized subprofessional occupations. The apprenticeships generally guarantee employment for a period of several critical years. In this country apprenticeships among teenagers seem to be about one-tenth as common—this despite the fact that the number of apprentices appears to be nowhere nearly adequate to supply our future needs for skilled workers; they will supply only about 31 per cent of the electricians needed, for example, 45 per cent of the tool and die makers, and only 10 to 25 per cent in most other trades.

Fortunately, we can claim that we are learning a great deal in the area of training. The Area Redevelopment Act of 1961 and the Manpower Development and Training Act of 1962 provide for short-term training and retraining under certain circumstances, and substantial training programs are under way as a result of these acts. But there is much yet to be done in this important field.

Effective placement. We are not newcomers in the field of placement. Our federal-state system has great accomplishments to its credit. This system, however, must overcome obstacles in the form of state boundaries, a problem with which most Europeans need not contend.

From another point of view, it appears that the personnel in some of our placement offices do not have as high a degree of professional competence as the personnel in certain foreign placement offices, for example those in Sweden.

Placement is an area in which the U.S.S.R. is quite ineffective, and it experiences considerable unemployment as a result. In a rather negative sense, therefore, we are able to learn something even from our chief cold-war adversary.

Relocation of industry and of workers. Many European countries, Great Britain and France in particular, have done a very effective job in inducing industry to locate or expand in surplus labor areas. A number of countries, including Sweden and the members of the Coal and Steel Community, have achieved considerable success in assisting workers to move from areas of heavy unemployment to places where job prospects are better. A great variety of inducements may be offered, such as payment of moving expenses, aid in disposing of a home, and aid in locating a new home. Although the worker's acceptance of the aids to worker mobility is entirely optional, the persuasion applied to industry frequently goes much further, involving selectivity in extension of credit, the granting of building permits, making energy available, and so forth.

In this country we have made a beginning toward the relocation of industry through our policy of awarding government contracts and through the Area Redevelopment Act and the Public Works Acceleration Act. All of these, of course, observe the principle of positive inducement, with acceptance on a strictly voluntary basis. Because of political opposition by communities reluctant to lose citizens and legislators unwilling to lose votes, we have made virtually no progress in encouraging geographic shifts on the part of workers stranded in economically stagnant communities.

Public planning and information. Many economists feel that the European countries could not have been as effective as they have been in combating unemployment without a considerable degree of public planning and control. The *Plan de Modernisation et d'Equipment* in France, the National Economic Development Council (NEDDY) in the United Kingdom, and the Royal Labor Market Board in Sweden are examples of different types of economic planning agencies that exercise a great deal of influence in channeling the national product into investment or consumption, determining the scope of public works and services, stimulating or restricting production in particular industries, establishing policy in vocational guidance and worker training, and so forth. The state itself is a very important employer in some countries, and as a matter of policy it can do much to offset fluctuations in employment in private industry. Thus in Sweden many workers in highly seasonal trades such as forestry and construction are enabled to enjoy practically full-time employment.

The highly controversial question of whether we should learn to do more planning will be left aside here. We shall move in that direction very slowly, if at all. Our own approach is to give to individuals a very high degree of discretion as to what they will produce, and how and where they will produce it. We have, therefore, responsibility to develop effective information about what is going on in our economy and to forecast to the very best of our ability the changes that can be expected to occur in the future. Statistics and research are highly important in a planned economy, but they are even more essential in one that is not planned.

Stimulating economic growth. These factors, however, can offer relatively little to the solution of our unemployment problems as compared with increased economic growth. Some of them are bound to look quite effective when the economy is rising rapidly, but all of them put together will not hold unemployment within bounds if our growth rate is lagging.

Every country tries to create the conditions favorable to economic growth. But there is no assurance that the policies that have worked in some European countries can be applied here. We suspect, moreover, that two important factors that help to account for the recent rapid growth of the European economies are conditions we would not want to see any closer at hand— gradual recovery from a devastating war and the delayed attainment of industrial maturity.

This is certainly not to suggest that a relatively mature industrial economy, unaffected by war's destruction, cannot maintain a sufficiently rapid rate of growth to utilize its manpower resources. But we have reason to doubt whether particular economic policies that have been applied in Europe would bring equally good results here under our very different circumstances. How much have they actually had to do with recent favorable economic trends in Europe?

Our own approach to economic policy for growth can take good advantage of Europe's experience, but own own policy must be made to measure. An early, substantial cut in business and consumer taxes will constitute a highly important forward step in the direction in which we should be moving.

Summary

Unemployment has been a much less serious problem in the industrial countries of Europe in recent years than here, but the lessons we can learn from their experience—and put to practical application—are distinctly limited.

Some of the problems we have faced have been present in Europe as well, but they have not prevented the countries of Europe from achieving relatively full employment. Some of the advantages enjoyed by European countries in the struggle against unemployment are clearly unattainable here. We shall want to take a long, hard look at some of Europe's defenses against unemployment, which we suspect may carry too high a price tag.

We have a good deal to learn, on the other hand, from Europe's experience with administrative programs, such as training and retraining programs, the relocation of industry, aids to worker mobility, and some aspects of labor placement. These programs are particularly effective in contending with structural unemployment. We need to know much more about these programs than we do, and to be prepared to adapt them to American conditions.

In the area of economic growth, too, we can profit from European experience, particularly from the courage and steadfastness with which some countries have followed an economic policy once it has been adopted. We will find, however, no convenient formula for economic growth. In that most important area of all we must work out our own salvation.

NOTES

1. Those interested in further detail are referred to *Measuring Employment and Unemployment* (Washington, D.C.: Government Printing Office, 1962), Chapter X and Appendix A. See also Joseph S. Zeisel, "Comparison of British and U. S. Unemployment Rates," *Monthly Labor Review*, May 1962.

2. See Zeisel, *op. cit.*

3. Both Italy and Japan suffer from a considerable amount of "underemployment," not reflected in the unemployment rate.

4. Revised.

5. See Edmund Nash, "Recent Trends in Labor Controls in the Soviet Union," in *Dimensions of Soviet Economic Power*, hearings together with a compilation of studies prepared for the Joint Economic Committee, Congress of the United States, 87th Cong., 2d sess., December 10 and 11, 1962, pp. 391–407 and pp. 691–693. The writer has also profited from an opportunity to review an unpublished manuscript on manpower in the U.S.S.R.

6. See, for example, the article by Edmund K. Faltermayer, "Labor Turnover, Cold Plague USSR Efforts to Develop Huge East," in *Wall Street Journal*, February 27, 1963.

7. See Arcadius Kahan, "Labor Turnover in the Soviet Union," *Monthly Labor Review*, January 1962. Kahan calls attention to Soviet materials indicating that some 36 to 60 per cent of the workers in 232 industrial plants studied may have changed jobs in 1960, and he suggests that the national average may have been near the lower end of this range. He estimates the average duration of unemployment for workers changing jobs at 28–31 days.

8. Displacement resulting from automation and increasing efficiency is also taking place constantly, although layoffs are often delayed until the worker can be transferred to another job. In such cases the result is a type of "underemployment" rather than unemployment, and the burden falls on the economy as a whole rather than on the individual worker.

9. All the countries exhibited marked seasonal fluctuations in production and employment, but only in the United States and Canada did economic growth show pronounced cyclical movements during this period.

10. See Zeisel, *op cit.*

Discussion

ROBBEN W. FLEMING

It may be that the problem of reducing unemployment in the United States is more political than economic, and that economists tend to give this fact too little attention. To illustrate the point, economists seem to agree that manipulation of the tax level is a far more effective weapon against unemployment than are public works or youth corps projects. Yet public works programs are politically viable, so far as Congress is concerned, while an effective tax program may not be.

If the day ever comes when we conclude that we have nothing to learn from the experience of other countries, particularly the democracies of Western Europe with which so much of our history is intertwined, it will be a sad day indeed. But it is not easy to transfer European experiences to this country. Perhaps we should stress not only our larger population and area, but, more significantly, our heterogeneity. This characteristic, coupled with the problems of federalism which make it so difficult, for instance, to have effective labor market controls on the Swedish pattern, should not be underestimated. Teachers of labor law are continually reminded that our difficulties in that field are multiplied by our efforts to apply a single national law to situations which are different in kind. This is not to suggest that a regional or local approach would be preferable, but rather that it is enormously difficult to construct a national law which must apply to dissimilar situations. In short, there is reason to agree with, and probably go beyond, Dr. Downie when he points out that, "The problem of reconciling the conflicts of different interest groups, which is what government is about, comes near to being different in kind when the population in question is raised by a factor of four and the area by one of fifteen."

Commissioner Myers has cleared away many of the collateral questions which tend to distract our attention from the more important and difficult issues of comparative unemployment. He has pointed out that a comforting statistical explanation of our relatively higher unemployment will not hold water. And he washes away such other easy explanations as different rates of growth in the labor force, more women or young people in the American labor force, and differences in structural unemployment.

On the purely informational level there are two points made by Commissioner Myers about which we might raise questions. The first relates to the issue of differing national attitudes toward job security, particularly layoffs. Myers concludes that the greater job security which is assumed to attach to the European worker is achieved at a very heavy cost. Those who have given a little attention to his problem doubt that the European worker does, in fact, enjoy more job security than his American counterpart. And, if he does, it is not at all certain that a close analysis would prove that this is achieved at a "very heavy cost." Professor Frederic Meyers of UCLA has been researching this point in Western Europe; his studies would not support a finding that workers in Western Europe enjoy more job security. Perhaps this is an area in which we need more information before any firm conclusions can be drawn.

As a footnote to this job security comment, a note of caution might be added on Japan. With respect to Japan Commissioner Myers says: "There is probably no country in the world where the worker who has attained permanent status has greater job security than in Japan. Many such workers enter their jobs directly from school and stay there until retirement."

The Myers statement is one which has long been supposed to be true. However, Professors Levine and Karsh of the University of Illinois have in recent years devoted an increasing amount of their time to the study of labor in Japan. They say that Americans are misinformed on the degree of job security in Japan, and that jobs are not nearly so secure as most American students of Japan seem to think.

The other point made by Commissioner Myers which may be worth some elaboration has to do with training and the relatively higher rate of apprenticeships in Europe than in America. He notes, for instance, that in Great Britain in a recent year about 35 per cent of the boys and 10 per cent of the girls getting out of school in that country were apprenticed to skilled crafts or undergoing training for recognized subprofessional occupations. But we must also keep in mind that European countries pay an extremely low apprenticeship wage during the early years. Such a wage is not one which would permit the person to live on his income, much less to support a family. How does one compare youth employment if the traditions of the countries are entirely different with respect to apprenticeship? To put it another way, if 35 per cent of the boys in Great Britain are apprenticed on getting out of school, but such apprenticeships are so low paying that the individual is not self-supporting, how does one compare this situation with that in United States?

Finally, with respect to what we can learn from training experiences in Europe, it should be noted that one of our most difficult and persistent problems has no real parallel in those countries. This is the race problem. Those who have experimented with retraining efforts in the South in private industry know the difficulties which are encountered when one tries to arrange for educational programs for Negroes if the available facilities happen to have been used for whites only.

For understandable reasons, Commissioner Myers has chosen to leave aside the controversial question of planning. On that score he says, "We shall move in that direction very slowly, if at all." We should be reluctant to drop the subject so quickly unless it can be said that there is no relationship between economic growth and planning, for most economists say that economic growth is the *sine qua non* of all employment. With the exception of West Germany, where it is arguable that a high rate of growth was inevitable in any event in the postwar years, it seems that most of the other Western European countries have engaged in one form or another of planning. If it is in fact essential to improvement of our situation, can we ignore it simply because it is controversial? Incidentally, it appears that the Italians are as allergic to the word "planning" as we are, but they have found a wonderful way out. The same thing can be discussed with complete equanimity if it is called "programming." Apparently computers have made that word completely respectable.

Dr. Downie seems to be aware of the problem which any government has in making its economic policies operative, but it may be that he underestimates the nature of the political problem in the United States.

Dr. Downie has said: ". . . there can be two quite different reasons why the performance of a government is responding inadequately to the demands of the situation with which it is faced. The government may be wrong or in doubt about what it ought to do. Or, knowing what it ought to do, it may be unable to do it because the governed do not accept that such action would in fact be 'in the national interest.' "

There is a third reason why the response of a government may be inadequate, and the third reason is the real reason in our case. The government may fail to respond despite the fact that it knows perfectly well what it wants to do and has the acceptance of the governed. It may fail because the governmental machinery is such that the initiative of the Executive and the support of the people do not meet a response in Congress. James MacGregor Burns has discussed this point with lucidity in his new book entitled *The Deadlock of Democracy*.

Dr. Downie has also said: "Having concluded that European countries had no pre-eminent advantages in respect to the task they faced [that is, bringing about full employment] or the capacities at their disposal, we are led to conclude, by exclusion, that the major reason why most of them have done better than the United States is that Europeans have been more determined that governmental capacities should be used. On this view, what European experience has to teach people in the United States is that people tend to get whatever it is that they want most."

The Burns book and Emmet John Hughes' *The Ordeal of Power*, which is a memoir partly devoted to the difficulties between the Executive and the Congress during the Eisenhower years, both emphasize the difficulty of getting what either the Executive or the people want through the Congress of the United States. Thus, when Dr. Downie says, ". . . although it may be argued that any administration in the United States has constitutional constraints on its freedom of maneuver to a degree unknown in Europe, experience suggests that these limitations are not decisive in practice when some course of action commands wide support," perhaps he takes the problem too lightly. Does experience really suggest that the limitations of our present deadlock between Executive and Legislative branches are not decisive when some course of action commands wide support? It does not seem to. Despite his unquestioned popularity with the people,

Franklin D. Roosevelt fought the Congress with only limited success after that first fateful 100 days. General Eisenhower, an enormously popular president, had relatively little success with Congress. President Kennedy did not score any momentous victories in the 1963 session of Congress. Is this because presidents have not known what they wanted, or because they were not backed by the people? Or is it because our party structure and the way in which we organize the Congress continually thwart the Executive and the majority of the people? The evidence is quite clear that it is the latter.

WILLIAM H. MIERNYK

Dr. Downie and Commissioner Myers have clearly shown that the governments of Western Europe have grasped some of the fundamental lessons of modern economics which have had little impact as yet on the United States. They have learned how to maintain a full employment level of effective demand or, in current terminology, an acceptable rate of economic growth. And they recognize that labor markets function imperfectly; that while an adequate level of effective demand is a necessary condition for full employment it is not sufficient. European governments have taken positive action to bring jobs to workers, or in some cases to move unemployed workers to job surplus areas.

Neither Dr. Downie nor Commissioner Myers is highly optimistic that the United States will learn much from European experience. However, we have already learned a great deal from Europe about labor market policy. There are European prototypes for the programs discussed by Commissioner Myers. The Area Redevelopment Act is similar to the British Local Employment Act of 1960. The Manpower Development and Training Act has a counterpart in Sweden. Efforts by the U. S. Employment Service to increase interstate labor mobility are similar to the co-operative programs of the European Coal and Steel Community and of Western European countries to encourage the movement of workers across national boundaries.

Commissioner Myers thinks Europe has had as much structural

unemployment as we have had, or possibly more. But the governments of Western Europe started to do something about it long before we did, and they have gone farther in attacking the problem. The labor market policies launched in the United States during 1961–1962 have not been operating long enough to show conclusively how much they will contribute to a solution of the unemployment problem. On the basis of what has happened in Western Europe, it would seem that those policies will make an important contribution if we can also meet the necessary condition of a full employment level of effective demand.

Dr. Downie finds little difference in the technical capacities of the United States and European governments to influence economic developments, and little difference in the ratio of taxes to national income on the two sides of the Atlantic. But, while the United States has the same capacity as Western Europe to achieve full employment, Dr. Downie concludes, it lacks the *will* to do so. This is the result of a difference in priorities. We are much more concerned about price stability than about full employment in this country. Why is this so? Possibly it is because price increases affect all of us while unemployment is distinctly a minority problem, and we do have a strong Benthamite bias in this country. But when Jeremy Bentham urged governments to seek the greatest good for the greatest number the poor and disadvantaged constituted a substantial majority. Rigid adherence to the utilitarian postulate in the affluent society, however, could perpetuate the culture of poverty recently dramatized by Michael Harrington in *The Other America*.

On the question of relative price stability versus full employment, Dr. Downie's analysis is not reassuring. His data show that consumer price increases in Europe have exceeded those in the United States and Canada—both high-unemployment economies —in every period for which he has made comparisons. And Dr. Downie feels that, given our present institutional constraints, price stability and full employment are incompatible. This, of course, is a rather widely accepted view. The Samuelson-Solow thesis [*] that average price increases and unemployment rates in the United States are inversely related suggests that we are faced

[*] Paul A. Samuelson and Robert M. Solow, *American Economic Review*, Vol. L, May 1960, p. 192.

with an ineluctable choice between creeping inflation or relatively high unemployment rates. The historical evidence seems to support this thesis, but it has not yet achieved the status of an inexorable economic law. Certainly, as Dr. Downie points out, price stability can be maintained only by constant and strenuous effort. But would it not be possible through judicious injections of funds to create employment in those sectors of the economy which have been hit hard by unemployment without unleashing general inflationary tendencies? In any event, if we do not have to make a choice, a modestly rising price level is not too high a price to pay for fuller utilization of our human resources.

We know quite a lot about the anatomy of unemployment in the United States thanks to the unremitting efforts of the Department of Labor. The first *Manpower Report of the President* contains detailed data on unemployment by age groups, sex, color, occupation, industrial attachment, location, labor force status, and duration. Probably no other country can match the quality of our labor statistics. But knowledge does not always lead to action. We have not gone as far as the countries of Western Europe in applying selective remedies. And we can still learn much from a country such as Sweden which, in spite of the problem of "wage drift," has kept price increases within tolerable limits while maintaining one of the lowest unemployment rates in the free world.

Commissioner Myers has summarized the major points in the report of the President's Committee to Appraise Employment and Unemployment Statistics. There can be no reasonable doubt that our unemployment rates are higher than those in Europe. But despite the report of the President's Committee the charge is still heard with discouraging regularity that America's "high" unemployment rate is a statistical mirage. Not only do many of our policymakers lack the will to do anything about unemployment, but also some of them are unwilling to accept it as a reality. If a few legislators continue to insist that unemployment is simply the result of erroneous definition of the labor force—or of unemployment—others will feel less inclined to support the policies needed to ensure full employment.

Americans have not learned, as Europeans have, that unemployment is costly. Commissioner Myers feels that we are sacrificing

$40 to $50 billion in goods and services annually by our failure to match European unemployment rates. Only a fraction of this amount would have to be spent on a selective basis to reduce unemployment substantially. And immediate and direct savings would be involved. Last year we spent over $3 billion on unemployment compensation alone. This figure would be cut in half if the unemployment rate in the United States could approximate that of Great Britain. There is not much point in suggesting that we try to match the rates found in Sweden, France, or West Germany.

If we are to achieve full employment, there will have to be some fundamental changes in attitudes. We will have to worry a little less about the "greatest number" in our society and a little more about the unemployed minority. The moral indignation of Americans has always been aroused by inflation. Recent events in Great Britain suggest that Europeans can become equally aroused by rising unemployment. In the United States, however, there is a vast indifference to unemployment among most of those not directly affected. We will not solve, or significantly mitigate, the unemployment problem in this country until there is more popular support for effective solutions.

There is some reason to question the conclusion that the lessons we can learn from Europe are limited. Why are European governments more responsive to the needs of a minority in the labor force than our own? Why are Europeans less timid than we are about pursuing expansionary fiscal policies? What differences in political processes and institutional arrangements permit European governments to pursue the goal of full employment without restraint while similar efforts in this country are regularly thwarted by the conservative coalition in Congress? What factors have contributed to the greater degree of understanding and co-operation between governments and business in Europe than in the United States? These questions deal less with economics than with social psychology and political behavior. Both Commissioner Myers and Dr. Downie have touched on them. But we need to know much more about these issues.

Surely the world's wealthiest nation can find ways to overcome present obstacles to full employment. And, if we do, many who now resist them might be surprised at the soundness of measures which would add to our gross output while reducing the cost of maintaining the unemployed. And such measures would have the useful side effect of restoring dignity to the minority group which has paid such a steep price for helping to maintain the rest of us in a state of relative affluence and apathy.

RICHARD A. LESTER

What general lessons can be drawn from Dr. Downie's and Commissioner Myers' comments?

The first is that the different experience in Europe to a significant extent rests on a difference in economic philosophy. As Dr. Downie explains, the European countries are less afraid to use governmental action in economic affairs and, in doing so, they put more stress on full employment and less on price stability than we have in this country. However, an active labor market policy and manpower planning, with stress on training and relocation allowances, generally relies on persuasion rather than compulsion or regulation.

Actually, in this country we seem to have at least as much control exercised by government in the labor market, but our action generally is piecemeal and unco-ordinated, perhaps because of our 50 states spread over a continental area. In Europe, on the other hand, there are *national* programs that are more clearly focused and better co-ordinated.

The second general conclusion to be drawn from the European employment experience of the past decade is that many of the explanations of our unemployment problem seem highly questionable in the light of European experience.

One explanation has run in terms of distortions in our wage structure. Lloyd Reynolds, in his elaborate study, *The Evolution of the Wage Structure* (1956), clearly demonstrates that the wage structures in countries like England, France, and Sweden are more subject to the charge of distortion, based either on job evaluation or market criteria, than they are in this country. The so-called "wage drift" in England and Sweden has not overcome the force of ideas of "wage solidarity" or traditional differentials.

Still another claim is that our system of unemployment compensation is responsible for a significant volume of unemployment. This belief is particularly surprising since experience rating in unemployment insurance was originally justified on the grounds that it would help to prevent unemployment. Professor Eckstein even proposes to make the range of tax rates more extreme than the present spread of 0.1 to 4 per cent of payroll. In a number of states the maximum tax rate is 10 to 20 times the minimum rate; to propose to make the spread any greater on grounds of unemployment prevention is most questionable both in theory and on the basis of past experience. We seem to overlook the fact that industries such as the automobile, steel, and rubber industries, have supplemental unemployment benefit programs in addition to the state benefits. However, the result of elaborate benefit programs has not so much been less unemployment as the encouragement of variation in hours, especially overtime, rather than the hiring of new employees. Pressures to prevent expansion of work forces when the nation's labor force is expanding so rapidly clearly operate in the wrong direction so far as the unemployment problem is concerned. That is also why, assuming that Commissioner Myers is correct when he says that European employers assume more responsibility for maintaining employees, the results may not be so helpful in reducing unemployment as he implies. A basic problem with our unemployment compensation system is that all the burden rests on employers' payrolls; that particular tax rests on mistaken notions about prevention.

Also, Commissioner Myers' argument about our unemployment benefits is based on absolute levels rather than on benefits relative to national wage levels, which is the relevant comparison. On that score, it is clear that our benefit levels are relatively low and do not cause workers to prefer to remain unemployed.

It should be clear that unemployment compensation would add to the total volume of unemployment only if it increased unfilled job openings by so restricting the supply as to expand the sum total of vacancies.

Turning now to the question whether our task of overcoming unemployment is essentially more difficult than that of European countries, the data presented to this conference seem to indicate that it is not. For example, on the demographic side, Commissioner Myers points out that, in terms of growth in the labor force, women in the labor force, and young workers in the labor force, our situation is as favorable as, or more favorable than, that of most European countries. Also, the *rate* of productivity increase, and probably the rate of increase in the application of technological change, have been as rapid in Europe as here. Only the marked decline of agricultural employment and the acute minorities problem would seem to be significant structural factors that aggravate our unemployment problem as compared with that of European countries.

There are some specific differences between this country's economic arrangements and those of European countries which, as the conference has brought out, may merit more emphasis and analysis than they have heretofore received.

One of these is tax structure. Dr. Downie shows that the central government in the United States obtains six times as much tax revenue from direct taxes on households and corporations as it does from indirect taxes. By contrast, the United Kingdom and Sweden derive about equal amounts from direct and indirect taxes, and Germany and France get more than twice as much from indirect as they do from direct taxes.

A second question for further investigation is "Why is our economy more recession-prone than that of European economies?"

A third question raised by Dr. Downie's remarks on ignorance of the national debt in Britain is whether some ignorance may not be an advantage. Maybe we too frequently compare minute changes in the thermometer. It might be a good thing if we could debunk the retail price index so as to show that small changes of fractions of a point are often meaningless and that quality changes may be enough to offset price changes. In any event, to make a change of one-tenth of a point in this index the subject of front page newspaper comment seems to exaggerate the figures out of all relationship to their actual importance or reliability.

Another difference that we might seriously consider is why our more widespread economic education has not resulted in more enlightened action. Compared to Europe, we have a much higher proportion of both the adult population who have had college courses in economics, and of academic economists per 100,000 population. Has education in economics made much difference, or has it been frustrated in terms of policy application by our fear of central government and our traditional notions about finance?

Essentially, then, what can we learn from foreign experience?

One clear-cut lesson is that the mental barriers stemming from our political philosophy and from our economic priorities are severe obstacles. As Dr. Downie says, we prefer price stability to reduced unemployment, in contrast to European countries.

Our mental barriers have also affected our willingness to plan for the labor market area. We fear government intervention there, too, even though such intervention may be designed to make the market operate more effectively by improving mobility, by adapting supply to demand, and by eliminating discriminations that block the most effective use of resources.

Clearly, there is a relationship between manpower planning and the rate of economic growth. And one of the lessons from abroad is that manpower planning is not something that can be done overnight. It is a long-term program, involving guidance in the secondary schools, developing qualified personnel in the public employment service, reducing some of the barriers to labor mobility, and so forth. Partly, it is a matter of influencing people's thinking and attitudes.

Basically, then, the difficulties in solving both the aggregate demand and the structural aspects of unemployment in this country are largely educational. We have to improve economic understanding and to stimulate action based on that understanding.

Perhaps we economists, including the labor economists, have been failing in our job. Perhaps we have not clearly discerned and stressed the lessons already learned. Perhaps we need to be a loud, clear voice forcefully explaining what needs to be done and how it can and should be accomplished.

CHAPTER **8**

Conclusions

BY ARTHUR M. ROSS

It is a time-honored cliché that economists never agree on anything. Yet the papers and comments given at the 1963 Conference on Unemployment and the American Economy reveal a surprising measure of agreement on the nature of the unemployment problem in the United States, the labor market programs which have been started during the past several years, and the fiscal policies necessary to stimulate economic growth. In addition to the conference's formal sessions there were several long, private discussion sessions among the 75 conferees; and in those sessions, too, the consistency of thinking was quite impressive, despite the varied affiliations of the group (academic, government, management, labor, journalism, and finance).

I was originally tempted to present this final chapter as a consensus of views of the conferees concerning national employment policy. But this might have been unwarranted exercise of editorial license, since some of the conferees might not have agreed with my version of the consensus. For this reason I present the following comments as my own editorial conclusions.

1. One of the most dangerous aspects of unemployment in the United States is that the nation does not consider it a very important problem. I say this despite much contrary evidence: unemployment is receiving more attention in 1964 than it received in 1958 or 1960. Not only did the Kennedy Administration give it more emphasis than the Eisenhower Administration did; but also the Negro protest movement, the railroad work-rules dispute, and the flood tide of young workers streaming into the labor market have deepened public awareness of unemployment. Furthermore, it is not really possible to characterize the attitude of the nation as a whole. For example, the Labor Department and the Council of Economic Advisers appear to regard the problem more urgently than the Treasury Department; the Executive seems more worried than the Congress; economists are more vexed than the general public. (Perhaps it is natural that economists, professionally concerned with the world of work, consider it particularly important that everyone should have an opportunity to work.)

But, in observing that we accept excessive unemployment as normal, I am really speaking about the results. We let it go on year after year, whereas we are galvanized into all-out action when the Russians move ahead of us in space exploration. Although the employment act has not been repealed, the implementation has certainly been feebler than one would have expected when the act was adopted in 1946. When the personal tragedies, the social problems, the economic losses and the labor-management conflicts resulting from unemployment are considered, it is clear that unemployment has not received the *effective* attention it deserves.

2. Explanations for this state of affairs are somewhat varied. Professor Rees, for example, attributes it to the balance struck between the competing objectives of full employment and price stability. In his view, an emphasis on price stability represents a poor appraisal of relative costs and benefits. Certainly Professor Rees is correct if he intends to describe the results of present U. S. economic policies: as compared with Western European countries, the country has had less employment or more price stability. Whether this represents a conscious or deliberate decision by the people as a whole is more difficult to say.

3. Dr. Downie stresses the tradition of noninterventionism in

American political ideology. In his view, the overriding American objective has been "the negative objective of avoiding strong and purposeful government of economic affairs." He states that "the major reason why most of [the European countries] have done better than the United States is that Europeans have been determined that governmental capacities should be used." Here again the explanation has an important germ of truth, but it should not be pushed too far. It is clear enough that industry and labor are opposed to controls which limit their freedom of action, and that Congressmen, as well as businessmen, are resistant to the idea of governmental planning. Yet opinion polls on aid to education, health insurance, and so on, do not reveal any deep-seated distrust of government among the general public. And even business anti-interventionism is highly selective. As A. A. Berle has observed,[1]

. . . Private corporations steadily assert that they do not want the government in business. They mean by this that they do not want the area of their economic power diminished. The same corporations are nevertheless frequently the first to demand that the government get into business when they feel their power position threatened by forces they themselves are unable to control. . . . Their objection therefore cannot be that exercise of economic power by the state is *per se* wrong.

In other words, noninterventionism is perhaps more a matter of strategy than of ideology and the weakness of employment policy can be traced to the political process.

4. Professor Fleming remarks that "the problem of reducing unemployment in the United States is more political than economic," and singles out Congressional immobilism for particular attention. The built-in conflict between legislative and executive branches of the government, the lack of discipline in American political parties, and the responsiveness of individual Congressmen to sectional and sectarian pressures are certainly undesirable. But, despite James MacGregor Burns's "four-party system," Congress is not the pre-Gaullist Chamber of Deputies. Congress moves quickly when it wants to, even in sensitive areas. Little time was lost in passing a compulsory arbitration law to settle the railroad work rules dispute in 1963.

Unemployed workers in general are politically passive. Others plead their case with some success, but they do not exercise political strength on their own. The majority of the unemployed are found among the less articulate segments of the population.[2] Furthermore, although social services in the United States are far below the level of luxury sometimes portrayed by imaginative editorial writers, nevertheless the unemployed are not actually starving. Left-wing radicalism is at a low ebb, and hence the agitational possibilities created by long-term unemployment are not exploited to any extent.

The unemployed are not only passive but also largely invisible. Suburbanization has brought about segregation by income level; unemployed workers tend to live in central city areas rather than in the suburbs where the more influential group have been migrating. In fact, in some areas such as Los Angeles, the unemployed are geographically separated from some of the newest and largest industrial plants and office buildings which have been located in the suburbs.[3]

5. Despite differences in emphasis, participants in the conference seemed to concur that the reduction of unemployment is an uphill struggle politically. The situation was similar with respect to the explanation of current unemployment: basic agreement with differences in shading. One could not find a pure structuralist, nor a pure aggregative theorist. Perhaps there is still a residual controversy as to whether certain kinds of structural differentials have increased in recent years. Nevertheless it is likely that most or all of the conferees would concur in the following propositions: (a) Whether or not the structural differentials have increased, they are certainly large and persistent. If a 6 per cent unemployment rate for the entire labor force is serious, the much higher rates for young persons, Negroes, and manual workers are intolerable. (b) No practicable expansion of aggregate demand would be sufficient to provide satisfactory employment opportunity for those groups who have the greatest disabilities in today's labor market. Even if it be conceded that deficiency in demand has been the real cause of higher unemployment since 1957, aggregative solutions will not suffice. (c) On the other hand, retraining the unemployed and other "structural" solutions will accomplish very little unless new jobs are created more rapidly. Thus, regardless of its etiology, the unemployment problem is both structural and aggregative from a practical standpoint.

6. Examining the statistics which are cited so liberally by the authors in this volume, one comes to realize that unemployed workers are still largely on their own. Many are eligible for unemployment compensation, it is true; but many are not. During 1962 total unemployment averaged about 4 million; the number of unemployed receiving compensation averaged 1,767,000. Thus less than half the unemployed have been getting insurance payments. In most states the maximum weekly payment is less than half of average weekly wages. All in all, the declining effectiveness of the unemployment insurance system serves as a vivid illustration of the low priority attached to the unemployment problem. The system is so badly underfinanced that reserves are below the "solvency level" in 23 states.[4] Although year-end reserves, as a proportion of total payrolls, have declined continuously from 6.6 per cent in 1951 to 2.9 per cent in 1962, the average payroll tax is only 1.3 per cent as compared with 2.7 per cent when the Social Security Act first went into effect.

The new manpower programs under ARA, MDTA, and the Trade Expansion Act are very significant policy developments, but only about 1 per cent of the unemployed workers obtain new jobs, and only a small proportion find them through the public employment offices. Most jobs are still secured by direct application or with the help of friends and relatives.[5] Thus, although the unemployed are not starving, it should not be thought that a benevolent government is smothering them in solicitude.

7. The new manpower programs have made a beginning in the development of a badly neglected segment of public policy. As Professor Somers states, "Regardless of any short-run deficiencies, there can be little doubt that retraining the unemployed is a worthwhile enterprise from the standpoint of the long-run economic growth of the American economy and the general well-being of its citizens. . . . Retraining allowances will usually take the place of unemployment compensation or relief payments for unemployed workers . . . in what better way can the unemployed spend their moments of enforced idleness than in the acquisition of new skills? . . . Retraining can give a new sense of pride, confidence and social status to unemployed workers; and these represent substantial social gains regardless of immediate labor market consequences."

Nevertheless, after about a year of experience we can see that there were exaggerated expectations concerning the new manpower programs. Retraining does not create jobs and is not a direct or immediate cure for unemployment. It produces workers who are qualified to fill new jobs if and when the jobs materialize. What is more, it is not practical to move unemployed workers into real "shortage occupations" through the medium of retraining courses limited to one year. Many of the shortage occupations are in the professional category and require an educational background which unemployed workers typically do not possess. In fact, a considerable proportion of the unemployed do not have enough education to be trainable as machine operators, store clerks, or stenographers.

Under these circumstances some changes are needed in concepts and assumptions underlying the federal retraining programs. Limiting instruction to immediate vocational skills provides no answer for the "hard core" of unemployed who need to acquire basic literacy before they can go further. Identification of training opportunities should be in terms of national manpower trends rather than short-run local labor market requirements. Older workers with limited skill can best be fitted into local service industries, it is true; but many of the younger workers can, and should, migrate to areas of industrial growth after their qualifications have been improved. Because of our rapidly changing technology, these younger workers may have to readjust themselves several times before reaching the age of retirement. In order to make them more adaptable, they should receive some general grounding in the basic sciences underlying the new technology.

8. If there is one principal idea which runs through most of the chapters in this book, it is that manpower policy must now be viewed as an entity rather than merely a congeries of loosely connected endeavors, and must be infused with a consistent and coherent strategy. On this point Professor Haber speaks for most of the authors: "The country sorely needs a national manpower program. Bits and pieces of such a program are strewn over the economic landscape. The heart of such a program must be full employment, however it is defined. Unless more jobs are developed, all other measures are palliatives which evade and avoid the only solution to unemployment consistent with a job economy.

We need also a labor market policy on a continuing basis. Too much of what we do had its origin during the great depression or has been created in response to an emergency. Our manpower resources cannot be neglected: millions left without adequate basic education; many ill equipped for the occupational requirements of these times and without proper counseling and direction. Perhaps, out of the present investigation into why we have unemployment during prosperity, we may begin to take the necessary steps toward the creation of a national manpower program."

9. The concept of national manpower policy is not very familiar in the United States because up to the present we have not been particularly conscious of the need for coordination of education, counseling, occupational training, income maintenance, worker migration, and other processes affecting the labor market. Changes in manpower needs, for example, the decline in agriculture and the growth in manufacturing, have proceeded gradually, so that the adjustment of the labor force has not been a difficult problem. American workers have been regarded as the most mobile of any in the world. Aside from the established professions, we have not emphasized formal qualifications and certifications for particular types of work. American political tradition has frowned upon economic planning and governmental intervention and has decreed that public activities be divided among local, state, and federal agencies with only a modicum of integration.

10. The concept of an integrated national manpower policy has many implications which can only be suggested here.[6] In the first place, there should be more emphasis on national, rather than merely local, manpower requirements in the planning of training programs. Secondly, retraining the unemployed should be viewed as only one phase in the upgrading of the labor force. The uneducated "hard core" must become literate before they are ready for occupational instruction. Unemployed workers can be moved up a few notches in skill but within a practicable range. Higher on the ladder, employed workers can be upgraded, through on-the-job training programs, into the newer and more technical occupations, leaving room on the lower rungs for the presently unemployed. But, since two to three million young people, many having excellent preparation, are coming into the labor market each year, this strategy of comprehensively upgrading the labor

force cannot work unless we have sufficient expansion of economic activity.

Privately operated training facilities are very extensive and are often superior, in quality of equipment and instruction, to the public vocational training institutions. They should be brought into the ambit of the national manpower policy. It is frequently noted that industry is training millions of employees whereas the government is training some 50,000 unemployed. But my own observation has been that even the industrial programs leave much to be desired. In particular, middle-aged production workers are not receiving instruction on new types of equipment and in new occupational specialties to a proper extent. As a result they find it difficult to qualify for promotional opportunities and are vulnerable to layoff when the old processes are phased out. As a matter of national policy, employers should be encouraged to broaden the qualifications of more of their existing employees. Moreover, arrangements can be made under which private employers would make their facilities and instructors available to train the unemployed. To bring employers into contact with the unemployed in this fashion could eventually lead to great changes in the operation of the labor market.

The concept of a national manpower policy raises other questions. Why should there be separate federal programs under ARA and MDTA, and still another "adjustment allowance" program under the Trade Expansion Act? Will formal apprenticeship programs ever be successful in producing more than a small percentage of skilled workers? [7] Should we not develop more information about how the great majority of skilled tradesmen become qualified? This might indicate what could be done by employers, unions, and government agencies—aside from apprenticeship—to increase the supply of skilled workers in the shortage trades. Should local vocational training programs be concentrated so heavily on the manpower needs of agriculture, our most rapidly declining industry? If the matching of labor demand and labor supply is viewed as a national objective, should we not do more to increase labor mobility? If the government makes special efforts to provide qualified workers for hospitals and other low-paid service activities, should it not require the employers to increase wages and improve working conditions in return for this assistance?

11. The question of relocation allowances deserves special comment. Allowances play an important and useful role in certain European manpower programs. In a few American industries, such as the railroads, financial assistance is provided displaced workers who take jobs in other communities. But it is well known that American workers are the most mobile of any in the world. Millions of families change their residence every decade, traveling on government-built highways for the greatest part. Is more help really justified? Young people with good education can and do move about the country, seeking better economic opportunity, without too much difficulty. There are many middle-aged workers, however, whose horizons are limited to their own county or state. They are not accustomed to travel and are reluctant to leave familiar surroundings. To move their children and household goods is an expensive operation. Unlike the young people, they cannot afford to shop around the country looking for a better place to settle down. The case for relocation allowances is that displaced middle-aged workers need special assistance or they are likely to vegetate and decay in areas where employment opportunity has permanently dried up.

12. The need to move workers into areas of greater opportunity implies that we will have only limited success in bringing additional employment to the distressed areas where stranded workers presently live; and our brief experience with ARA tends to confirm this expectation. The incentives which can be offered to private industry under the terms of the act are not powerful enough to attract large enterprises which otherwise would locate elsewhere. There would certainly be great resistance if the government should attempt to impose some of the stronger controls on industrial location which have been used in Sweden and Britain; in fact, even the notion that employment conditions should be taken into account in awarding government contracts has provoked so much controversy that the Department of Defense has proscribed this criterion altogether. All of this means that, for the most part, workers will have to follow the work. Just as the operating railroad brotherhoods cannot succeed in pre-

serving pre-existing levels of employment in their crafts, communities such as Johnstown, Pennsylvania, Wheeling, West Virginia, and Lowell, Massachusetts, cannot succeed in holding together their pre-existing population. They *should* lose population, in line with geographical shifts in economic opportunity. Thus the concept of a *national* manpower program means that, although training, counseling, and other manpower services will be provided in localities through local agencies, nevertheless the strategical objective is to reconcile changing patterns of labor demand and labor supply in the *national* economy. This, of course, is easier said than done.

13. The labor market field is a particularly complicated maze of local, state, and federal authorities and private interest groups which have to be persuaded, accommodated, or displaced before new programs can be launched or old ones changed: Department of Labor; Department of Commerce; Department of Health, Education and Welfare; state employment service and unemployment compensation officials; state and local education authorities; the vast apparatus of apprenticeship committees; organized labor; the business community. It must be recognized that these public and private vested interests, all having their own specialized points of view, make up a peculiarly difficult context within which to implement an integrated national manpower policy. There is a natural tendency to use existing facilities and personnel, including local employment service and vocational training officials with their limited horizons. In the absence of a dramatic national crisis, it is not likely that the established apparatus will be by-passed and a new structure established. Under these circumstances, advocates of an integrated manpower program will have to make large compromises with reality for many years to come.

14. Another thought which is iterated and reiterated throughout this book is that labor market policies will accomplish little or nothing unless more strenuous efforts to restore full employment are made. The Kennedy Administration's principal effort to stimulate the economy in 1963 has been the proposed income tax reduction. Congress has been asked to vote a $10 billion reduction in personal and corporate taxes, to take effect in three stages over an eighteen-month period, along with a number of

tax reforms. At the Conference on Unemployment and the American Economy this proposal was thoroughly reviewed both in the formal sessions and the informal discussions. Considering the diverse origins and convictions of the 75 conferees, the extent of agreement was quite remarkable. There was a clear (although certainly not unanimous) accord on the following propositions: (a) an income tax cut is an urgent necessity. (b) Controversy over some of the contemplated reforms should not be permitted to delay the reduction in rates. (c) The reduction should be on the larger rather than the smaller side. (d) It should be scheduled to take effect more rapidly rather than more slowly. (e) It should be concentrated among low- and middle-income receivers. (f) It might be strategic, at some later date, to enact a further tax reduction for high-income groups, along with the proposed reforms. (This thought is based on the fact that the high-income groups presently benefit most from the practices to be reformed.)

At the end of 1963, final action on the tax bill was put off until the following year, and it seemed clear that the reduction would not be sufficiently large, sufficiently rapid, or properly distributed to have the full impact which is desirable. This verifies our conclusion that the priority attached to full employment, while improving, is still too low.

I wish to conclude these observations with a thought I cannot claim to have derived entirely from the other chapters in the book. In the middle of the twentieth century there have been two overriding developments in the American economy: first, the kaleidoscopic changes in technology, occupational structure, industrial location, and other aspects of economic activity; and, second, the more exacting standards of performance to which the economy is subject. Thus the context is more difficult and the objectives more demanding. Unless some of the objectives (such as high employment) are to be sacrificed, I think it is clear that there will have to be more extensive economic planning in the future than we are accustomed to now.

The concept of economic planning is not a popular one in this country. For this reason we will not call it economic planning when (and if) we develop it. Furthermore it will be our own brand. It will not be the same as Soviet Russia's highly centralized totalitarian planning, or Yugoslavia's looser variety of communism, or Sweden's "middle way," or French-style planning through "modernization commissions," or the economic development plans of many newer Asian and African countries. It will have to be consistent with American geography, politics, and historical traditions.

Before an American version of economic planning can materialize, there will have to be an understanding between the federal government and the principal interest groups with respect to objectives, methods of implementation, and consultative mechanisms; and, before such an understanding can be developed, there will have to be a better relationship between American business and the government. Regardless of which party is in power, the present relationship is certainly not conducive to an effective full employment program. Communication is carried on in rather primitive clichés which do not encourage a real confrontation of the policy issues. Business and government operate with different systems of economic doctrine (while labor has yet a third); and, although the United States undoubtedly has more economists per capita than any other country, it cannot be said that the educated public is sophisticated on economic questions. An administration which attempts to innovate boldly in the economic field creates a crisis of business confidence which threatens to dry up the flow of private investment. A business-oriented administration, on the other hand, tends to pursue deflationary policies which reduce production and employment as the price of retaining confidence. Endeavors to develop more intimate consultation between government and business, or to engage in even the most informal "indicative" planning along Western European lines, cannot succeed if the parties must deal at arms length in an atmosphere of suspicion. One of the most crucial tasks of economic statesmanship in the coming generation will be to build a more mature relationship between government and business.

NOTES

1. A. A. Berle, *Power Without Property* (New York, 1959), p. 95.
2. However, the Negro protest movement is directed against unemployment as well as other disabilities.

3. This cloak of invisibility seems to surround not only the unemployed but other disadvantaged groups as well. Recent studies have shown that while one-third of the nation is no longer ill-fed, poverty is still surprisingly extensive in our affluent society (see Michael Harrington, *The Other America* (New York, 1962)). Certainly it comes as a shock to learn that "in 1959 almost every eighth family in the [San Francisco] Bay Area was living in poverty or deprivation." (Margaret Greenfield, *Social Dependency in the San Francisco Bay Area*, Berkeley, 1963, p. 1.)

4. Reserves are considered at the "solvency level" when they are sufficient to pay benefits for 18 months under recession conditions.

5. Wilcock and Franke, in a series of five case studies of plant shutdowns, reached a similar conclusion. "In general, the workers received little help from public employment service, company or union . . ." *Unwanted Workers* (Free Press of Glencoe, 1963), p. 125.

6. See E. Wight Bakke, *A Positive Labor Market Policy* (New York, 1903).

7. There are more than 8,000,000 "craftsmen, foremen and kindred workers" in the United States, but only about 150,000 apprentices. The bulk of the apprentices are in building-trades occupations.

Index